PRIMER OF
BOOK-KEEPING

ANSWERS TO
PRIMER OF BOOK-KEEPING

*Containing worked answers to all the exercises
in the Primer.*

PITMAN

JAMES HYNES

PRIMER OF
BOOK-KEEPING

An Introductory and Preparatory Course
of lessons in the principles of Book-keeping.
With exercises, list of business terms,
and specimen commercial forms.

DECIMALIZED EDITION

PITMAN PUBLISHING

Revised 1970
Reprinted 1972
Reprinted 1972
Reprinted 1974
Reprinted 1976

PITMAN PUBLISHING LTD
Pitman House, Parker Street, Kingsway, London WC2B 5PB
PO Box 46038, Portal Street, Nairobi, Kenya

PITMAN PUBLISHING PTY LTD
Pitman House, 158 Bouverie Street, Carlton, Victoria 3053, Australia

PITMAN PUBLISHING CORPORATION
6 East 43rd Street, New York, NY 10017, USA

SIR ISAAC PITMAN (CANADA) LTD
495 Wellington Street West, Toronto M5V 1G1, Canada

THE COPP CLARK PUBLISHING COMPANY
517 Wellington Street West, Toronto M5V 1G1, Canada

© Sir Isaac Pitman and Sons Ltd., 1970

ISBN 0 273 43943 X

Text set in 10/11 pt. Monotype Baskerville, printed by letterpress,
and bound in Great Britain at The Pitman Press, Bath
(B.846:46)

PREFACE

IN the present work an attempt is made to set forth the principles of double-entry book-keeping in the clearest and simplest manner possible, though nothing essential to a proper understanding of the subject has been omitted. The student who works carefully through the exercises in this elementary book will be prepared to enter upon the study of the more elaborate treatises intelligently, and with a thorough apprehension of the principles of the art. The books here explained are those which are common to almost every business, and it will be seen that they have been taken in the order in which they would, most likely, be required.

The questions have been arranged so as to form a revision of each chapter, and, along with the exercises, will be found sufficient to give the student a complete grasp of each principle. The answers to the questions will be found in the chapters at the end of which the questions appear, and the answers to the exercises are contained in *Answers to Primer of Book-keeping.*

CONTENTS

CHAPTER I

THE CASH BOOK

Book-keeping is the art of *recording business transactions* in a systematic manner, so that the books will show, at any time, the exact state of their owner's affairs.

The principles of Book-keeping are always the same, though their application differs according to the nature of the business. If, therefore, the principles of the art are thoroughly mastered, it will be an easy matter to adapt them as occasion may require.

A **Debtor** IS ONE WHO OWES; A **Creditor** IS ONE TO WHOM SOMETHING IS OWING. In business, that which is owing is always *money* or *goods*. In Book-keeping, the *receiver* of goods or money is always considered as the debtor, and the *sender* of the goods, or the *payer* of the money, is always considered as the creditor. It is, therefore, easy to tell whether a person is a debtor or a creditor by asking the question, "Has he *received* or has he *sent* the goods or money?" and the answer will show which of the two he is, so far as that particular transaction is concerned. Notice that in answering this question you are to think only of the transaction which has just taken place, without reference to anything which may have happened previously. If you *receive* money you are *debtor* for the amount, even though the person paying it owed you the money. If you *pay* money you are *creditor* for the amount, though you may be simply repaying what you borrowed the day before. It will be seen, however, that every transaction involves *both* a debtor and a creditor, and that there cannot be one without the other, for where there is a *receiver* there must be a *sender* or a *payer* also.

Everyone knows something about the receipt and payment of money; therefore, the **Cash Book,** in which receipts and payments of cash are recorded, will be most easily understood by the learner. Moreover, when we quite understand how to keep the Cash Book, we shall have gone a long way towards understanding how to keep the other books as well. So we will take the Cash Book first.

All the cash which is *received* is entered on the *left side* of the book, which is called the *debtor* (or debit) side, because, as we have seen above, the *receiver* is always considered as the *debtor*. All the cash which is *paid away* is entered on the *right side* of the book, which is called the *creditor* (or credit) side, because the *payer* or *sender* is always considered as the *creditor*. The two sides of the Cash Book form a page or **folio.**

Besides the outer column in which the cash received or paid is entered, the Cash Book contains an inner column on each side, in which the *discount* is entered. **Discount** *is the sum often deducted from an account, and usually for prompt settlement.* When we receive an amount the sum received is entered in the cash column on the **Dr.** (debtor) side of the Cash Book, and the *discount*, if any, allowed by *us*, is entered in the discount column on the *same side*; when we pay an amount, the sum paid is entered in the cash column on the **Cr.** (creditor) side of the Cash Book, and the *discount*, if any, allowed *to us*, is entered in the discount column on the *same side*. Entries on the **Dr. side** can be preceded by the word "*To*"; and those on the **Cr. side** by the word "*By*."

Now let us apply these rules and construct a Cash Book from the particulars in Ex. 1, remembering that the *receiver* is always *debtor*, and the *payer* always *creditor*; and that the discount must appear on the *same side* as the amount of cash received or paid.

On 1st Jan., Edward Keane commences business with £500 in cash. This is called his **capital,** and is *what he is worth* at this date. Mr. Keane invests this amount in the business; it is, therefore, a receipt from him, and it is accordingly entered on the Dr. side. "To E. Keane (Capital) £500." On 2nd Jan., £400 is paid into the Bank. A Bank is a place where money is put for safe keeping on the understanding, of course, that the whole or part may be taken out when wanted. There are also other advantages belonging to an account at a Bank,

EXERCISE 1

19..		£
Jan 1	Edward Keane commenced business with cash . .	500·00
2	Paid into Bank	400·00
8	Paid H. Harper	51·06
	Was allowed discount	2·69
9	Received cash from E. Cleaver	10·60
	Allowed him discount	0·28
11	Paid C. Taylor	28·50
	Was allowed discount	1·50
18	Received from G. Gray	17·84
	Allowed him discount	0·46
	Paid A. Armstrong	37·63
	Was allowed discount	1·98
	Drew from Bank	60·00
19	Paid T. Atkins	45·74
	Was allowed discount	2·41
20	Paid into Bank	10·00
22	Received from W. Hope.	20·00
30	Paid Rent	5·00
	Paid Wages	9·78

but you will learn more about them later on. This item is a *payment* and is, therefore, entered on the Cr. side, "By Bank, £400." And so on with all the others. When all the entries have been made, they should appear as under, with the exception of the figures in the narrow columns, which will be explained later.

Dr.   EXERCISE 1   **Cr.**

19..			£	£	19..				£	£
Jan 1	To E. Keane				Jan 2	By Bank .	19		400·00
	(Capital)	18		500·00	8	H. Harper .	19	2·69	51·06
9	E. Cleaver .	19	0·28	10·60	11	C. Taylor .	19	1·50	28·50
18	G. Gray .	19	0·46	17·84	18	A. Arm-			
	Bank . .	19		60·00		strong .	19	1·98	37·63
22	W. Hope .	19		20·00	19	T. Atkins .	20	2·41	45·74
					20	Bank . .	19		10·00
					30	Rent . .	20		5·00
						Wages .	20		9·78

QUESTIONS

1. What is a Debtor? A Creditor?

2. How can you tell whether a person is Dr. or Cr.?

3. Which is the Dr. side of the Cash Book? On which side are payments entered?

4. What is Discount? Which is the Discount Column?

5. On which side of the Cash Book would you enter discount allowed by you?

6. On Monday I borrowed £50 from W. Brown, and I paid him back on Wednesday. State the entries in the Cash Book for Monday and Wednesday.

EXERCISES ON CHAPTER I

From the following particulars compile a Cash Book, with Discount entered in the Discount columns.

EXERCISE 2

			£
19..			
Feb	1	J. Jones commenced business with cash	400·00
	2	Paid into Bank	350·00
	4	Received from T. Brown	10·50
	8	Paid G. Evans	15·00
	18	Drew from Bank	40·00
	19	Paid S. Sharp	80·44
		Was allowed discount	2·06
	25	Received from B. Barnett	14·63
		Allowed him discount	0·38
	26	Received from T. Baynes	0·77
	28	Paid Wages	8·38
		Paid Rent	4·25

EXERCISE 3

			£
19..			
Mar	1	J. Taylor commenced business with cash	450·00
	2	Bought Goods for cash (Cr. Cash "By Purchases")	50·00
	5	Sold Goods for cash (Dr. Cash "To Sales")	25·00
	8	Received from J. Jackson	9·75
		Allowed him discount	0·25
	10	Paid E. Eastwood	38·00
		Was allowed discount	2·00
	14	Bought Goods for cash	65·75
	17	Received from A. Armley	29·25
		Allowed him discount	0·75
	18	Sold Goods for cash	50·00
	24	Paid F. Farley	16·58
		Was allowed discount	0·43
	26	Received from H. Gornall	5·50
	31	Paid Trade Expenses (Cr. Cash "By Profit and Loss, Trade Expenses")	9·53

CHAPTER II

BALANCING THE CASH BOOK

Now we understand that all receipts are entered on the Dr side of the Cash Book, and all payments on the Cr. side. A very little thought will show us that the amount on the Dr side must never be less than that on the Cr. side, for we cannot pay away more than we have received. The difference between the two sides is called the Balance, and represents the amount we should have in hand after deducting the payments from the receipts. To balance the Cash Book, therefore,

EXERCISE 4

19..			£	£	19..			£	£
Jan 1	To E. Keane (Capital)	18		500·00	Jan 2	By Bank .	19		400·00
9	E. Cleaver .	19	0·28	10·60	8	H. Harper .	19	2·69	51·06
18	G. Gray .	19	0·46	17·84	11	C. Taylor .	19	1·50	28·50
	Bank .	19		60·00	18	A. Armstrong .	19	1·98	37·63
22	W. Hope .	19		20·00	19	T. Atkins .	20	2·41	45·74
					20	Bank .	19		10·00
					30	Rent .	20		5·00
						Wages	20		9·78
					31	Balance c/d .			20·73
			0·74	608·44				8·58	608·44
19.. Feb 1	To Balance b/d		29	20·73				29	

find the difference between the two sides, and place the amount on the Cr. side, on the line following the last entry, and opposite the words "By Balance." The two sides of the book will now be equal, and the totals should be placed under their respective columns, in a line with each other, and ruled off, as in the example. If the entries on one side do not come as low as those on the other side the space may be filled by ruling in the way shown above.

The Cash Book is usually balanced at the end of each month,

and the balance on the last day of one month forms the first entry for the first day of the following month. For instance, in Exercise 4, the balance is £20·73, and against the word "balance" we write in ink the letters "c/d," an abbreviation for "carried down," to show that the amount has been carried down as the first entry for February. In the same way, opposite the entry for 1st Feb., we put the letters "b/d," an abbreviation for "brought down," to show that the amount has been brought down from the preceding month. Note that the balance is always carried to the *opposite side*. The discount is *not* balanced, but simply added up and the amount placed under the discount column.

Now balance Exercise 1, as explained, and compare the result with Exercise 4.

QUESTIONS

1. Which side of the Cash Book must total more than or the same as the other, and why?

2. What is the balance? How do you find it?

3. Where do you enter the balance at the end of the month?

4. What do you do with the discount?

5. To which side do you always carry the balance?

6. Give the Cash Book entries for the following transactions:

    (*a*) Paid W. Kesley £5·70. Was allowed discount 30p.

    (*b*) Received from A. Lamb £9·50. Allowed discount 50p.

    (*c*) Paid Water Rate £3·63.

    (*d*) Borrowed £5·25 from S. Baines.

    (*e*) Lent J. Bird £2·60.

    (*f*) Received from J. Bird £1·53.

EXERCISES ON CHAPTER II

Compile and Balance Cash Book, showing Discount Received and Paid.

EXERCISE 5

19..		£
Apr 1	C. Hacking commenced business with cash	300·00
2	Paid into Bank	250·00
4	Paid D. Davis	23·75
	Was allowed discount	1·25
10	Bought Goods for cash	10·00
12	Sold Goods for cash	5·75
15	Drew from Bank	50·00
16	Paid H. Mason	19·50
	Was allowed discount	0·50
	Bought Goods for cash	40·00
30	Paid Trade Expenses	4·28

EXERCISE 6

19..		£
May 1	Cash in hand (*Dr.* Cash "To Balance")	50·00
3	Received from G. Freeman	48·75
	Allowed him discount	1·25
10	Paid J. Hope	57·00
	Was allowed discount	3·00
14	Bought Goods for cash	20·50
16	Received from A. Gill	5·50
20	Paid W. Wood	4·75
	Was allowed discount	0·25
30	Paid Trade Expenses	3·50

EXERCISE 7

19..		£
Jun 1	Cash in hand	10·83
2	Received from B. Good	66·50
	Allowed him discount	3·50
3	Paid into Bank	70·00
5	Received from H. Brown	20·00
6	Paid A. Dewse	15·75
8	Bought Goods for cash	10·00
10	Sold Goods for cash	15·00
14	Paid E. Walters	7·53
30	Sold Goods for cash	12·60
	Paid Wages	15·48

CHAPTER III

THE PURCHASES BOOK

WHEN we buy goods we receive, either along with the goods or through the post, an **Invoice,** *which is a list which gives particulars of the quantity and prices of goods sold.* When the goods are received they are examined to see that they agree with the particulars on the invoice. The invoice itself is always kept for reference When we buy the goods on *credit* that is to say, on *trust,* to be paid for at a later time, the particulars on the invoice are copied into a book, which is therefore, called the **Invoice Book,** the **Bought Book,** or, as we have called it, the **Purchases Book.** *The Purchases Book, then, is the book in which we record our purchases on credit* When we buy goods *for cash,* that is, when we pay for them *at once,* the transaction is *not* recorded in the Purchases Book.

The Purchases Book is sometimes ruled with double cash columns on the right-hand side of each page, and a *single* line on the left-hand side, so that there is a wide margin on the extreme left. The wide margin on the left is used for entering the page or folio of the Ledger to which the entry has been transferred. This will be fully explained later on, and for the present may be passed over. In the broad space to the right of the single line is placed the name of the firm from whom the goods have been bought, with the description and price of the articles. In the inner column is put the amount of each item, and in the outer column the total amount of the invoice. The name of the month, and the year, are written on the top of each page. The date of the purchase is placed above each entry, and a line ruled on each side of the figure.

Some book-keepers fold the original invoices and paste them in the Purchases Book, with the name, date, etc., written on the back of the invoice. Where this is done it is only

SPECIMEN INVOICES

TELEGRAPHIC ADDRESS:
MITRE, WOLVERHAMPTON
TELEPHONE: 16345

Mitre Street,
Wolverhampton

25th Jan. 19..

Mr. J. Axtel

Bought of DEWEY & SONS

TERMS: 2½% for Cash in month following delivery

1 Brass Umbrella		
Stand, No. 697	12·50 –	
20%	2·50 –	
		10·00
1 Crate		0·10
		10·10

76 Deal Street,
Manchester

2nd Jan., 19..

Mr. E. Keane

Dr. to H. HARPER

TERMS: 2½% one month

20 Yards Black		
Cloth @ £1·75	35:00	
15 Yards Brown		
Cloth @ £1:23	18:75	
		53·75

necessary to place the amount of the invoice opposite the
name of the seller of the goods. This method has many
advantages to recommend it. It saves a good deal of time
in copying out the details of the goods. Another method is
to enter the date, name of seller and total amount of the
invoice in the Purchases Book and file the original invoices
in special binders. It is easy to refer to any particular invoice
in case of dispute, and as they are the original invoices there
is no possibility of error in copying the particulars. The cash
columns are added up, the amount being placed at the foot
of each page and then carried forward to the top of the
next page. The sum at the end of the month represents the
total amount of goods purchased on credit for the month.

Where the business is a large one it is still more necessary
to save as much time as possible, and, therefore, instead of
copying the invoices, or pasting them into the Purchases
Book, each invoice when received would have a number
stamped on it and would then be put away in order of the
numbers in a special set of drawers called a Filing Cabinet.
In making the entries in the Purchases Book, the date of the
transaction would be placed first, then a column for the
number of the invoice; the name of the firm from which
the goods were bought would be shown next. Then would
come a small column for the Ledger page number; while
last of all would be the two money columns, as in the following
specimen—

Date	Inv. No.	PARTICULARS	Led. Fol.		

For the present, follow the plan illustrated in the specimen ruling and construct a Purchases Book from the following statement—

EXERCISE 8

19..		
Jan 2	Bought of H. Harper, Manchester	
	20 yards Black Cloth	@ £1·75
	15 ,, Brown ,,	@ £1·25
4	Bought of C. Taylor, Rochdale	
	5 pairs Blankets	@ £6·00
6	Bought of A. Armstrong, Leeds	
	1 doz. Shawls	@ £2·43 each
	5 ,,	@ £2·09 ,,
12	Bought of T. Atkins, Manchester	
	10 yards Sheeting	@ £1·25
	15 ,, ,,	@ £1·88
	Trimmings, £7·45	
24	Bought of H. Harper, Manchester	
	25 yards Black Cloth	@ £0·49

When the preceding particulars have been properly entered your Purchases Book should appear as follows—

Date	Inv. No.	Particulars	Led. Fol.		Amount
19..					£
Jan 2	10	H. Harper, Manchester	23		53·75
4	11	C. Taylor, Rochdale	23		30·00
6	12	A. Armstrong, Leeds	24		39·61
12	13	T. Atkins, Manchester	24		48·15
24	14	H. Harper, Manchester	23		12·25
		Total for the month	24		183·76

QUESTIONS

1. What is an Invoice?

2. What is a Purchases Book?

3. What do you mean by "Bought on Credit"?

4. Explain the uses of the two cash columns in the Purchases Book.

5. What other method do you know of treating Invoices?

EXERCISES ON CHAPTER III

Compile Purchases Books from the following statements—

EXERCISE 9

19..
Feb 1   Bought of S. Sparrow, London
             Cloth £50·53, Velvet £60·50 .   .   .
      3   Bought of W. White, Leeds
             Blankets £20·75, Quilts £30 .   .   .
      6   Bought of A. Headley, Manchester
             Prints £80·53, Twills £20   .   .   .
     15   Bought of T. Terry, Liverpool
             Silks £10·78, Satins £10·28   .   .   .
     20   Bought of Peel, Oram & Co., Manchester
             Grey Cloth £95·76, Remnants £5 .   .

EXERCISE 10

19..
Mar 1   Bought of T. Riley, London
             Flour £56·50   .   .   .   .   .
      5   Bought of G. Heywood, London
             Oats, £10   .   .   .   .   .   .
             Wheat, £85·00   .   .   .   .   .
     19   Bought of A. Harris, Liverpool
             Flour, £18·50   .   .   .   .   .
             Oats, £10·63   .   .   .   .   .

EXERCISE 11

19..
Apr 1   Bought of T. Hardy, Manchester
             5 yards Cloth A3 @ £2·13   .   .   .
             7   ,,   ,,   B7 @ £2·25   .   .   .
      8   Bought of S. Hanes, Manchester
             50 yards net @ 12p   .   .   .   .
             20 ,,   ,, @ 10p   .   .   .   .
     17   Bought of G. Slater, London
             20 yards Cloth C2 @ 75p   .   .   .
             Trimmings for £2·50   .   .   .   .
     30   Bought of J. Howe, Burnley
             Cloth A3 for £15·75   .   .   .   .

CHAPTER IV

THE SALES BOOK

WHEN we sell goods on credit, the date, the name of the buyer, with the particulars and prices of the goods, are entered in a book which is called the **Day Book,** or the **Sales Book.** The Sales Book, *therefore, is the book in which we record our sales on credit.* When we sell goods for ready money, the transaction is *not* recorded in the Sales Book.

The Sales Book is ruled exactly like the Purchases Book. The entries, too, are made in precisely the same way, the only difference being that they are records of *Sales* instead of *Purchases.*

The learner should have no difficulty, therefore, in compiling a Sales Book from the following statement—

EXERCISE 12

19..		
Jan 3	Sold to E. Cleaver, Bolton	
	4 yards Black Cloth	@ £2·13
	2 ,, Brown ,,	@ £1·18
10	Sold to G. Gray, Oldham	
	4 pairs Blankets	@ £3·63
	3 Shawls	@ £1·26 each
13	Sold to W. Hope, Stockport	
	3 pairs Blankets	@ £3·00
	4 Shawls	@ £2·64 each
	6 yards Black Cloth	@ £1·99
26	Sold to E. Cleaver, Bolton	
	5 yards Black Cloth	@ £2·13
	3 ,, Velvet	@ £2·38
	Trimmings for £1·21	
30	Sold to G. Gray, Oldham	
	2 yards Black Cloth	@ £2·00
	5 Shawls	@ £1·05 each

When entered, the foregoing particulars should appear in the Sales Book as shown on page 14

Date	Inv. No.	Particulars	Led. Fol.		Amount
19..					£
Jan 3		E. Cleaver, Bolton	26		10·88
10		G. Gray, Oldham	26		18·30
13		W. Hope, Stockport	26		31·50
26		E. Cleaver, Bolton	26		19·00
30		G. Gray, Oldham	26		9·25
		Total for the month	27		88·93

AN ORDER

Order No. 346 *49 Market Street,*
Manchester

3rd March, 19..

To THE COUNTY CHEMICAL COMPANY,
CLAYTON.

Please supply the undermentioned Goods and charge to our
account :—

Ten tons of Green Copperas, in
Casks about 5 cwt. each, @ £2·75
per ton.
To be delivered at Beswick
Station, to our order.
B. & C. Cooper.

QUESTIONS

1. What transactions are recorded in the Sales Book?

2. How is the Sales Book ruled?

3. In which column do you enter the total amount of each sale?

4. Would you enter a sale of goods for ready money in the Sales Book?

EXERCISES ON CHAPTER IV

Compile Sales Books from the particulars below—

EXERCISE 13

19..
May 1 Sold to N. Hough, London
      Flour, £33
   9 Sold to S. Garratt, Liverpool
      Oats, £5·63
      Wheat, £58·50
  17 Sold to H. Dean, Liverpool
      Flour, £100
      Wheat, £36
  31 Sold to T. Swann, Liverpool
      Flour, £5·50

EXERCISE 14

19..
Jun 1 Sold to Bennett & Co., Hull
      Wine, £125
        ,, £56·25
  10 Sold to Braine Bros., London
      Sherry, £80
      Port, £50
  18 Sold to Stephenson & Co., Liverpool
      Sherry, £48; Port, £56; Brandy, £100
  30 Sold to A. Richards, Dublin
      Sherry, £60; Port, £70; Brandy, £30

EXERCISE 15

19..
Jul 1 Sold to D. Seaton, Manchester
      Coal, £8·25
        ,, £1·23
  12 Sold to J. Wilson, Bolton
      Coal, £31
        ,, £28
  20 Sold to Vickers & Sons, Oldham
      Coal, £90
  29 Sold to Heaney Bros., Bury
      Coal, £60

CHAPTER V

THE LEDGER

POSTING THE CASH BOOK

THE **Ledger** is the most important of all the books used in business, for it contains an abstract of every transaction recorded in the other books. The Cash Book, Purchases Book, Sales Book, are called "subsidiary" books, or sometimes "Books of Original Entry," and are used largely to facilitate the entries in the Ledger, and to obviate the necessity for long statements in this important book. Really, the Cash Book is part of the Ledger, being the Cash Account taken out and bound up in a separate cover for convenience. All the transactions which have been recorded in the other books are arranged under convenient heads and entered in the Ledger, in the order of their dates. *The Ledger, therefore, is the book to which all the entries in the other books are posted, or transferred.* The ruling of the Ledger will be seen in the specimen pages.

In the chapter dealing with the Cash Book, we saw that every transaction involved both a debtor and a creditor, and that there could not be one without the other, for a receiver implied also a giver or sender. In making the entries in the Cash Book, however, we only took notice of *one* of these, the debtor or the creditor, but not *both*. For example, in Exercise 1, when we received £500 from Mr. Keane we considered ourselves as debtors to him for this amount, because we had *received* it, and the receiver is always considered as the debtor. The amount was, therefore, entered on the Dr. side of the Cash Book. But, if we were *debtors* because we *received* this sum, then Mr. Keane must have been the *creditor*, because he *paid* it, and the payer is always considered the creditor. Of this latter fact, however, at the moment, we took no heed. Again, when we paid £400 into the bank, we considered ourselves as creditors because we had paid it, and the amount

16

was accordingly entered on the Cr. side of the Cash Book. But, once more, if we were creditors because we *paid* the money, the bank must have been the debtor for this amount because it *received* it. And so on with all the other entries in the Cash Book. Though there are two sides to every transaction, up to the present we have taken note of only *one* side. Now, in the Ledger, we are about to supply these omissions. Take the Dr. side of the Cash Book first.

On 1st Jan., we received £500 from Mr. Keane, and we debited (debit, to put on the Dr. side of an account) the Cash Book with this amount. At the top of a page in the Ledger write "E. Keane, Capital Account." On the left side of the page put the abbreviation for debtor, "Dr."; and on the right side of the page the abbreviation for creditor, "Cr." As Mr. Keane *paid* the amount he is creditor, and so we credit (credit being to put on the Cr. side of an account) his account as follows: "Jan. 1st. By Cash, £500." To show where this amount has come *from*, put in the narrow column to the left of the cash column, the figure 3, which is the number of the page or folio of the Cash Book where the first entry appears. The narrow column is, therefore, called the *folio* column. In the same way, in the folio column of the Cash Book, and opposite to Mr. Keane's name, put down the page of the Ledger to which the £500 has been posted. Thus, in a moment we can see in the Cash Book where the amount has been posted *to*, and in the Ledger where it has been posted *from*. The folios here used are the pages of this book, where the references will be found.

Now, we have taken note of both sides of this transaction; we have debited the Cash Book because it received, and we have credited Mr. Keane's account because he paid the amount. Do the same thing with the other items which appear on the Dr. side of the Cash Book in Exercise 1, opening an account for the Bank, and for each of the persons named, and crediting these accounts with the respective amounts. Notice that where we have allowed these persons *discount* we must give them credit for the amount of the discount, as well as for the amount of the cash. For instance, on 9th Jan., E. Cleaver paid us £10·60 in cash, and we allowed him a discount of 28p; in posting this item into the Ledger we must write, "By Cash £10·60," and underneath this "By Discount 28p," as otherwise the amount on the Cr. side of the Ledger would not equal the amount on the Dr. side of the Cash Book, and this would land us into a difficulty later on.

When all the entries on the Dr. side of the Cash Book have been posted in the Ledger, take those on the Cr. side, and open a separate account for H. Harper, C. Taylor, A. Armstrong, and T. Atkins. There is already an account opened for the Bank. Instead, however, of having a separate account for Rent and Wages, put both these items under the heading of "Profit and Loss," as in the specimen on page 20. On the Dr. side of each account put down the amount which appears opposite the person's name on the Cr. side of the Cash Book. If we think for a moment, we shall see that *entries which appear on the* Dr. *side of the Cash Book are posted to the* Cr. *side of the Ledger, while entries which appear on the* Cr. *side of the Cash Book are posted to the* Dr. *side of the Ledger.* This is, in fact, the rule, and in this way we take note of both sides of each transaction appearing in the Cash Book.

Notice, also, that when a person allows *us* discount we must debit him with the amount of the *discount* as well as the amount of the cash we pay. Thus, when we paid H. Harper on 9th Jan., £51·06 in cash, he allowed up £2·69 as discount, and when posting this item into the Ledger, we must say, "To Cash £51·06," and underneath this, "To Discount £2·69," as is done in the specimen.

When all the accounts have been opened in the Ledger they should appear as follows—

EXERCISE 16

Dr.			E. KEANE, CAPITAL ACCOUNT		Cr.
			19.. Jan 1 By Cash . .	3	£ 500·00

Dr.				E. CLEAVER, BOLTON			Cr.
				19.. Jan 9	By Cash . Discount	3 3	£ 10·60 0·28

Dr.				G. GRAY, OLDHAM			Cr.
				19.. Jan 18	By Cash . Discount	3 3	£ 17·84 0·46

Dr.					BANK ACCOUNT		Cr.
19.. Jan 2 20	To Cash . ,, .	3 3	£ 400·00 10·00	19.. Jan 18	By Cash .	3	£ 60·00

Dr.				W. HOPE, STOCKPORT			Cr.
				19.. Jan 22	By Cash .	3	£ 20·00

Dr.			H. HARPER, MANCHESTER				Cr.
19.. Jan 8	To Cash . Discount	3 3	£ 51·06 2·69				

Dr.			C. TAYLOR, ROCHDALE				Cr.
19.. Jan 11	To Cash . Discount	3 3	£ 28·50 1·50				

Dr.			A. ARMSTRONG, LEEDS				Cr.
19.. Jan 18	To Cash . Discount	3 3	£ 37·63 1·98				

Dr.			T. ATKINS, MANCHESTER				Cr.
19.. Jan 19	To Cash . Discount	3 3	£ 45·74 2·41				

Dr.			PROFIT AND LOSS ACCOUNT				*Cr.*

19..			£				
Jan 30	To Cash (rent)	3	5·00				
	,, (wages)	3	9·78				

QUESTIONS

1. What is the Ledger?

2. To which side of the Ledger do you post entries which appear on the Dr. side of the Cash Book?

3. How would you enter in the Ledger discount which has been allowed *to* you?

4. What is the use of the folio column?

EXERCISES ON CHAPTER V

From the following statements compile a Cash Book, open a Ledger, and post Cash Book items to it—

EXERCISE 17

		£
19..		
Jan 1	Cash in hand (*Cr.* Capital Account "By Cash") .	200·00
2	Paid into Bank	160·00
5	Received from J. Watson	97·50
	Allowed him discount	2·50
8	Paid G. Baker	47·50
	Was allowed discount	2·50
12	Received from A. Finch	10·50
14	Paid into Bank	80·00
18	Paid G. Baker	19·50
	Was allowed discount	0·50
25	Received from J. Watson	15·36
	Allowed him discount	0·39
30	Paid Wages (*Dr.* "Profit and Loss") . . .	10·28

EXERCISE 18

		£
19..		
Feb 1	Commenced business with cash	600·00
2	Paid into Bank	300·00
	Bought Goods for cash (*Cr.* Cash, and *Dr.* Purchases	
	Account in Ledger)	250·00
4	Sold Goods for cash (*Dr.* Cash; *Cr.* Sales) . .	200·00
12	Received from H. Hughes	40·00
18	Paid C. Turner	20·00
28	Paid Trade Expenses (*Dr.* "Profit and Loss") . .	4·20

EXERCISE 19

								£
19..								
Mar	1	Cash in hand	.	.	.	.	.	5·78
	2	Received from B. Bailey.	.	.	.	.	.	45·00
	4	Paid W. Johnson	.	.	.	.	.	25·50
	8	Received from A. Youde	.	.	.	.	.	15·75
	12	Paid F. Farmer	.	.	.	.	.	5·25
	18	Received from A. Youde	.	.	.	.	.	2·50
	25	Received from B. Bailey.	.	.	.	.	.	15·00
	30	Paid Wages .	.	.	.	.	.	7·48

CHAPTER VI

POSTING THE PURCHASES BOOK

In posting the Cash Book, we saw that the entries on the Dr. side were posted to the Cr. side of the Ledger, because the persons who paid us money were our *creditors* for the amounts they paid. In the same way, when persons *send us* goods, for which we have not paid at once, they are our creditors for the value of the goods they send. The goods we buy in this way (on credit) are entered, as we have seen, in the Purchases Book, and in posting the entries from the Purchases Book into the Ledger we enter the amounts on the Cr. side of the person's account from whom we bought the goods, because he *sent* the goods, and the *sender* is always the *creditor*. *The Purchases Book, then, is posted to the Cr. side of the Ledger.*

Now turn to the Purchases Book in Chapter III, and you will see that we have already opened accounts in the Ledger for the persons there named. On the Cr. side of each person's account enter the amount of each purchase, with the date, and, in the folio column, the page of the Purchases Book where the entry appears. Preface each entry with the words "By Purchases Book." Then, in the folio column of the Purchases Book, put down the page or folio of the Ledger to which the amount has been posted. When this has been done we shall have given each person *credit* or the value of the goods he sent us.

So far, however, we have no *debit* entry for these goods in the Ledger, and to supply this we open an account called the "Purchases Account." The total amount of the goods bought for the month is £183·75, and because these goods were *received*, we *debit* the "Purchases Account" with this amount, in accordance with the rule that the *receiver* is always *debtor*. On the Dr. side of "Purchases Account," therefore, write "Jan. 31 To purchases, as Purchases Book, £183·75."

Now we have a *debit* and a *credit* for each amount in the Purchases Book, and our Ledger should appear as follows—

Dr.				E. KEANE, CAPITAL ACCOUNT			Cr.
				19.. Jan 1	By Cash .	. 3	£ 500·00

Dr.				E. CLEAVER, BOLTON			Cr.
				19.. Jan 9	By Cash . Discount .	. 3 . 3	£ 10·60 0·28

Dr.				G. GRAY, OLDHAM			Cr.
				19.. Jan 18	By Cash . Discount .	. 3 . 3	£ 17·84 0·46

Dr.				BANK ACCOUNT			Cr.
19.. Jan 2 20	To Cash . ,, .	. 3 . 3	£ 400·00 10·00	19.. Jan 18	By Cash .	. 3	£ 60·00

Dr.				W. HOPE, STOCKPORT			Cr.
				19.. Jan 22	By Cash .	. 3	£ 20·00

Dr.				H. HARPER, MANCHESTER			Cr.
Jan 19.. 8	To Cash Discount	. 3 . 3	£ 51·06 2·69	19.. Jan 2 24	By Purchases Book ,, ,,	11 11	£ 53·75 12·25

Dr.				C. TAYLOR, ROCHDALE			Cr.
19.. Jan 11	To Cash Discount	. 3 . 3	£ 28·50 1·50	19.. Jan 4	By Purchases Book	11	£ 30·00

Dr.				A. ARMSTRONG, LEEDS		Cr.
19.. Jan 18	To Cash . Discount .	.	3 3	£ 37·63 1·98	19.. Jan 6 By Purchases Book 11	£ 39·61

Dr.				T. ATKINS, MANCHESTER		Cr.
19.. Jan 19	To Cash . Discount .	. .	3 3	£ 45·74 2·41	19.. Jan 12 By Purchases Book 11	£ 48·15

Dr.				PROFIT AND LOSS ACCOUNT	Cr.
19.. Jan 30	To Cash (rent) ,, (wages)	. .	3 3	£ 5·00 9·78	

Dr.				PURCHASES ACCOUNT	Cr.
19.. Jan 31	To Purchases as Purchases Book .	.	11	£ 183·75	

QUESTIONS

1. Where do you enter goods bought on credit?

2. To which side of the Ledger do you post the Purchases Book?

3. Why is this?

4. To which side of the Purchases Account do you transfer the total amount of goods bought?

5. Under what rule do you do this?

EXERCISES ON CHAPTER VI

Ex. 20. Post into the Ledger the Purchases Book you compiled from Exercise 9 in the Exercises on Chapter III, opening a Purchases Account, and debiting it with the total of goods bought. Also, of course, open accounts for each person named in the exercise.

Ex. 21. Do the same with Exercise 10 in the same chapter.

Ex. 22 Do the same with Exercise 11 in the same chapter

CHAPTER VII

POSTING THE SALES BOOK

In posting the Cash Book we transferred the amounts which appeared on the Cr. side to the Dr. side of the Ledger, because the persons to whom we paid the cash were our *debtors* for the amount they received. Exactly in the same way, when we send *goods*, for which we are not paid at once, the persons to whom the goods are sent are our debtors for the value of the goods. The goods sold in this way (on credit) are entered in the Sales Book, and in posting the entries from the Sales Book into the Ledger we enter the amounts of the Dr. side of the person's account to whom we sold the goods, because he *received* them, and the *receiver* is always *debtor*. *The Sales Book, therefore, is posted to the Dr. side of the Ledger.*

On referring to the Sales Book in Chapter IV, we shall find that we have already opened accounts in the Ledger for the persons there mentioned. Now, on the Dr. side of each person's account, enter the amount of each sale, with the date and folio of the Sales Book where the entry appears, and preceded in each case by the words, "To Sales Book." In the folio column of the Sales Book, put down the folio of the Ledger to which the amount has been transferred. When this is completed we shall have *debited* each buyer with the amount of his purchase.

The total amount of the goods *sold* for the month is £88·93, and because these goods were *sent out*, we *credit* the "Sales Account" with this amount, under the rule that the *sender* is always *creditor* On the Cr. side of "Sales Account," then, write "Jan. 31 By Sales, as Sales Book, £88·93."

We have now a *debit* and a *credit* for each entry in the Sales Book, and when the posting is completed our Ledger will appear as follows—

Dr. E. KEANE, CAPITAL ACCOUNT *Cr.*

					19.. Jan 1	By Cash	.	.	3	£ 500·00

Dr. E. CLEAVER, BOLTON *Cr.*

19.. Jan 3 26	To Sales Book " "	. .	14 14	£ 10·88 19·00	19.. Jan 9	By Cash Discount	. .	. .	3 3	£ 10·60 0·28

Dr. G. GRAY, OLDHAM *Cr.*

19.. Jan 10 30	To Sales Book " "	. .	14 14	£ 18·30 9·25	19.. Jan 18	By Cash Discount	. .	. .	3 3	£ 17·84 0·46

Dr. BANK ACCOUNT *Cr.*

19.. Jan 2 20	To Cash "	. .	. .	3 3	£ 400·00 10·00	19.. Jan 18	By Cash	.	.	3	£ 60·00

Dr. W. HOPE, STOCKPORT *Cr.*

19.. Jan 13	To Sales Book	.	14	£ 31·50	19.. Jan 22	By Cash	.	.	3	£ 20·00

Dr. H. HARPER, MANCHESTER *Cr.*

19.. Jan 8	To Cash Discount	. .	. .	3 3	£ 51·06 2·69	19.. Jan 2 24	By Purchases Book " "	11 11	£ 53·75 12·25

Dr. C. TAYLOR, ROCHDALE *Cr.*

19.. Jan 11	To Cash Discount	. .	. .	3 3	£ 28·50 1·50	19.. Jan 4	By Purchases Book	11	£ 30·00

Dr. A. ARMSTRONG, LEEDS *Cr.*

19.. Jan 18	To Cash Discount	. .	. .	3 3	£ 37·63 1·98	19.. Jan 6	By Purchases Book	11	£ 39·61

Dr.   T. ATKINS, MANCHESTER   Cr.

19..					19..			
Jan 19	To Cash	.	3	£ 45·74	Jan 12	By Purchases Book .	11	£ 48·15
	Discount .	.	3	2·41				

Dr.   PROFIT AND LOSS ACCOUNT   Cr.

19..								
Jan 30	To Cash (rent)	.	3	£ 5·00				
	,, (wages)	.	3	9·78				

Dr.   PURCHASES ACCOUNT   Cr.

19..								
Jan 31	To Purchases as Purchases Book	.	11	£ 183·75				

Dr.   SALES ACCOUNT   Cr.

					19..			£
					Jan 31	By Sales as Sales Book .	14	88·93

QUESTIONS

1. To which side of the Ledger do you post the Sales Book? Why is this?

2. With what words do you precede each entry?

3. To which side of the Sales Account do you transfer the total amount of goods *sold*? Under what rule is this done?

4 What do you mean by *Debit*; and by *Credit*?

EXERCISES ON CHAPTER VII

Ex. 23. Post into the Ledger the Sales Book you compiled from Exercise 13 in the Exercises on Chapter IV, opening a Sales Account, and crediting it with the total amount of goods sold for the month. Open accounts, also, for each of the persons mentioned in the Sales Book.

Ex. 24. Do the same with Exercise 14 in the same chapter.

2

CHAPTER VIII

DOUBLE ENTRY

THE TRIAL BALANCE

WITH one exception, we have now a *debit* and a *credit* in the Ledger for each item which appears in the Cash Book, Purchases Book, and Sales Book, counting the Cash Book, of course, as part of the Ledger for all the items concerning cash.

The one exception is the Discount allowed *by* us and *to* us. This exception we will fill in now.

On referring to our Cash Book, we find that we have allowed to others discounts amounting to £0·74. This we may regard as a *loss*, since it has reduced our profits by this amount, and the item is, therefore, entered in that account which represents our losses and gains, namely the "Profit and Loss Account." This account is *debited* with our *losses*, and so in the "Profit and Loss Account," on the Dr. side, enter "Jan. 31. To Discounts, as per Cash Book, £0·74." The Cr. side of the Cash Book shows that discounts amounting to £8·58 have been allowed *to* us. This we look upon as a *gain*, and accordingly we enter the amount on the Cr. side of the "Profit and Loss Account," because we *credit* this account with our *profits*. It will be seen, therefore, that discounts are transferred to the *same* side of the "Profit and Loss Account" as that on which they appear in the Cash Book. The folio of the Cash Book appears in the Profit and Loss Account against the item "Discounts" as usual, but when we show the corresponding page number of the Profit and Loss in the Cash Book, instead of putting the number 29 in the narrow column as before, where it might apply to either the total of the "Discount" or that of "Cash" column, we show it immediately underneath the Discount total as shown on page 5.

The "Profit and Loss Account" will appear as shown on page 29.

Dr.				PROFIT AND LOSS ACCOUNT			*Cr.*
19..			£	19..			£
Jan 30	To Cash (rent) .	3	5·00	Jan 31	By Discounts as per		8·58
31	,, (wages) .	3	9·78		Cash Book .	5	
	Discounts as per						
	Cash Book .	5	0·74				

If we think now for a minute, we shall see that we have *two entries* in the Ledger for every transaction we have had in our business; we have a *debit* and a *credit* for each entry; in other words, we have kept our books by **Double Entry**. Let us review the facts, and we shall find this is so.

When we received money, we *debited* the Cash Book with the amount, and *credited* the payer's account in the Ledger.

When we paid money, we *credited* the Cash Book with the amount, and *debited* the receiver's account in the Ledger.

When discount was allowed *to* us by others, we *debited* their accounts with the amount, and we afterwards *credited* the "Profit and Loss Account" with the total amount thus allowed. When discount was allowed *by* us to others, we *credited* their accounts with the amount, and we afterwards *debited* the "Profit and Loss Account" with the total amount thus allowed.

When we *bought* goods, the particulars were entered in the Purchases Book. At the end of the month, we *debited* "Purchases Account" with the total amount of goods received; while we *credited* each sender's account in the Ledger.

When we *sold* goods, we entered the particulars in the Sales Book, and at the end of the month we *credited* the "Sales Account" with the total amount of goods sold; while we *debited* each buyer's account in the Ledger.

The great advantage of the Double Entry is that it tends to prevent mistakes by *testing the accuracy of the posting*. It has other advantages as well; for instance, it enables a merchant to keep separate accounts for the various branches of his business, and to ascertain the profits or losses resulting therefrom; it shows, at once, the details of his trading, and enables him to compare the state of his business, at any time, with the corresponding period in any previous year, and so helps to guide his actions for the future.

Let us now test the accuracy of our posting. If every *debit* has a corresponding *credit*, it follows that the total of the debits should equal the total of the credits. To ascertain if this is so, we make out what is called a **Trial Balance**. This is done as follows—

Rule a sheet of paper with double cash columns (or a page of the Cash Book will answer the purpose), and write out a list of the accounts which appear in the Ledger. Find the total amount on the Dr. side of each account, and put it down in the *inner* column, which is called the Dr. column. Do the same with the Cr. side, putting the amount in the *outer* column, which is called the Cr. column. Where it is found that both sides of an account are the same, it is useless putting the amount in the Trial Balance, as, of course, it would not affect the result either way. Proceed thus until you have taken in all the accounts in the Ledger. There will still remain one other account to be included, and that is the one in the Cash Book. Take the total of the Dr. side of the Cash Book and insert it in the inner column, and then put the total of the Cr. side in the outer column. Add up both columns of the Trial Balance, which should then show an equal amount in each column. When the Trial Balance is completed, compare it with that given below.

TRIAL BALANCE

	Dr. £	Cr. £
E. Keane (Capital Account)		500·00
E. Cleaver	29·88	10·88
G. Gray	27·55	18·30
Bank	410·00	60·00
W. Hope	31·50	20·00
H. Harper	53·75	66·00
Profit and Loss Account	15·51	8·57
Purchases Account	183·75	
Sales Account		88·93
Cash Book	608·44	587·70
	1,360·38	1,360·38

This method is shown you so that the *principle* of the Double Entry can easily be seen; but in actual business practice the "Totals" method, as it is called, of making a Trial Balance is not often used, a shorter method being preferred. This shorter method is called the "Balances" method, and consists in finding the difference between the two sides of the account, and then in the Trial Balance placing that difference in the column, Dr. or Cr., which represents the larger side. For instance, in E. Keane's Capital Account the credit side is obviously the larger side because it has £500 entered in it, and nothing on the debit. Therefore, we place £500 in the Cr. column of the Trial Balance against E. Keane's name In E. Cleaver's Account we can see that the difference between the two sides is £19, and the debit side has a greater amount than the credit, therefore we place the amount, £19, in the debit column, and so on with the rest of the accounts. When the differences are all found and entered, the two columns should be added up, and then, if your arithmetic is correct and the entries correctly made, the two totals should agree. The following shows how the previous example would appear when made according to the "Balances" method.

TRIAL BALANCE

	Dr. £	Cr. £
E. Keane (Capital Account)		500·00
E. Cleaver	19·00	
G. Gray	9·25	
Bank	350·00	
W. Hope	11·50	
H. Harper		12·25
Profit and Loss Account	6·94	
Purchases Account	183·75	
Sales Account		88·93
Cash Book	20·74	
	601·18	601·18

QUESTIONS

1. To what account do you transfer the total amount of discount allowed by you, or to you?

2. What is Double Entry? What is its great advantage?

3. How do you prove the accuracy of the posting?

EXERCISE ON CHAPTER VIII

EXERCISE 25

From the following particulars compile Cash Book, Purchases Book, Sales Book, and Ledger. Post the first three books into the Ledger, and draw out a Trial Balance

19..			£
Jan 1	Commenced business with cash		1,000·00
2	Paid into Bank.		800·00
4	Bought of W. Hall, Cloth £100, Velvet £50·50 .		150·50
6	Sold to C. Bate, Cloth £40·28, Velvet £10·72 .		51·00
8	Paid W. Hall, £142·98. Was allowed discount £7·52		150·50
13	Received from C. Bate £49·73. Discount allowed £1·27		51·00
14	Bought Goods for Cash (Cr. Cash; Dr. Purchases Account)		50·00
16	Sold Goods for cash (Dr. Cash; Cr. Sales Account)		45·00
18	Sold to C. Bate, Cloth £10·53, Velvet £20 .		30·53
20	Bought of W. Hall, Cloth £150, Velvet £30. .		180·00
24	Sold to T. Keate, Cloth £5·53, Velvet £3 . .		8·53
28	Bought of G. Moore, Prints £70 . . .		70·00
	Received from C. Bate		20·00
	Paid W. Hall		80·00
30	Paid Trade Expenses		15·93

CHAPTER IX

BALANCING THE LEDGER

WE have now posted everything into the Ledger, and it only remains for us to find out whether we have lost or gained on our month's transactions. This is done by balancing the Ledger.

The student will remember that in balancing the Cash Book (Chapter II) the method was to find the *difference* between the two sides, and place it on the lesser side, so as to make both sides equal, and that the *difference* was called the *balance*. We balance the Ledger in the same way. Observe this one rule, however; always leave the Capital Account till the *last*, and the Profit and Loss Account till the *last but one.* The reason of this will appear as we go on.

Begin, then, by balancing the accounts of E. Cleaver, G. Gray, Bank, W. Hope, H. Harper, C. Taylor, A. Armstrong, and T. Atkins.

Before balancing the accounts for goods let us consider them a moment. We have bought goods to the amount of £183·75; we have sold goods amounting to £88·93. Now, it is on the sale of goods that we make a profit or suffer a loss. But the difference between the two amounts just named will not represent our profit or loss. Why? Because we have a considerable quantity of goods still *unsold*, and which must be taken into account. Let us take an example. I buy four watches for £10. Three of them I sell at £3 each, and receive therefore, £9. But I have still *one* watch unsold, which is worth (at *cost* price) £2·50. It is clear that before I can say whether I have gained or lost on my watches, I must take into consideration the watch I have still left. If I put this into the form of an account it would appear as on the following page.

So it is with our accounts for goods. Before we can *balance* we must find the worth of the goods we have still *unsold* In

Dr.		WATCHES ACCOUNT		*Cr.*
	£			£
To Cash (Cost of four Watches) .	10·00	By Cash (for three Watches sold) .		9·00
Balance (Profit) . . .	1·50	Watch unsold (Cost Price) .		2·50
	11·50			11·50

actual business this is done by stock-taking; that is, finding the quantity of goods unsold, and calculating their value at *cost* price, or at the market price of the day. In our case, we will suppose the goods remaining unsold to be worth £109·65, and this amount we put on the Cr. side of a Trading Account. The balances of our Purchases and Sales Accounts are transferred to this account. The debit entry for stock is in a new account headed Stock Account. *Now* we find the difference between the two sides of the account to be £14·83, and this represents our *gross* profit on the goods sold during the month. This amount is transferred to the account which represents our net profits or losses, viz. the Profit and Loss Account, and as the balance came out on the Dr. side of Trading Account it is carried to the Cr. side of Profit and Loss Account, because balances always *cross over*.

In the Trading Account, therefore, we write on the Dr. side, "Jan. 31. To Balance transferred to Profit and Loss, £14·83"; and in the Profit and Loss Account we write, "Jan. 31. By transfer from Trading Account, £14·83." The Trading Account may now be ruled off, as in the specimen given on page 37.

Now we come to the balancing of the Profit and Loss Account, which is done by finding the difference between the two sides, and transferring it to the Capital Account. This difference represents the *net* profit on the month's working. In other words, to make the profit of £14·83 on the goods, it *cost* us £14·78 in *expenses*, so that our profit on goods is reduced by this amount. Further, we have allowed to *others* discounts amounting to £0·73, which, as we have previously pointed out, may be regarded as a *loss*. Against this, however, we may set down as a *gain* the £8·57 which has been allowed to *us* in discounts. Our net profit, therefore, is £7·89, which is the balance of Profit and Loss Account, and as this amount increases the CAPITAL which Mr. Keane first put into the business, it is transferred to Mr Keane's Capital Account, as shown in the example.

Lastly, we come to the Capital Account itself, which is balanced by finding the difference between the two sides, and carrying that difference *down* as the first entry for February.

When all the accounts have been balanced, the Ledger will appear as follows.

Dr.   E. KEANE, CAPITAL ACCOUNT   *Cr.*

19..				£	19..				£
Jan 31	To Balance	.	c/d	507·89	Jan 1	By Cash	.	3	500·00
					31	Transfer from Profit & Loss (Net gain)	.	37	7·89
				507·89					507·89
					Feb 1	By Balance	.	b/d	507·89

Dr.   E. CLEAVER, BOLTON   *Cr.*

19..				£	19..				£
Jan 3	To Sales Book	.	14	10·88	Jan 9	By Cash	.	3	10·60
26	,, ,,	.	14	19·00		Discount	.	3	0·28
					31	Balance	.	c/d	19·00
				29·88					29·88
Feb 1	To Balance	.	b/d	19·00					

Dr.   G. GRAY, OLDHAM   *Cr.*

19..				£	19..				£
Jan 10	To Sales Book	.	14	18·30	Jan 18	By Cash	.	3	17·84
30	,, ,,	.	14	9·25		Discount	.	3	0·46
					31	Balance	.	c/d	9·25
				27·55					27·55
Feb 1	To Balance	.	b/d	9·25					

Dr.   BANK ACCOUNT   **Cr.**

				£					£
19.. Jan 2 20	To Cash ,,	.	3 3	400·00 10·00	19.. Jan 18 31	By Cash Balance	.	3 c/d	60·00 350·00
				410·00					410·00
Feb 1	To Balance	.	b/d	350·00					

Dr.   W. HOPE, STOCKPORT   **Cr.**

				£					£
19.. Jan 13	To Sales Book	.	14	31·50	19.. Jan 22 31	By Cash Balance	.	3 c/d	20·00 11·50
				31·50					31·50
Feb 1	To Balance	.	b/d	11·50					

Dr.   H. HARPER, MANCHESTER   **Cr.**

				£					£
19.. Jan 8 31	To Cash Discount Balance	. . .	3 3 c/d	51·06 2·69 12·25	19.. Jan 2	By Purchases Book ,, ,,	11 11		53·75 12·25
				66·00					66·00
					Feb 1	By Balance	.	b/d	12·25

Dr.   C. TAYLOR, ROCHDALE   **Cr.**

				£				£
19.. Jan 11	To Cash Discount	. .	3 3	28·50 1·50	19.. Jan 4	By Purchases Book	11	30·00
				30·00				30·00

Dr.   A. ARMSTRONG, LEEDS   **Cr.**

				£				£
19.. Jan 18	To Cash Discount	. .	3 3	37·63 1·98	19.. Jan 6	By Purchases Book	11	39·61
				39·61				39·61

Dr. T. ATKINS, MANCHESTER **Cr.**

			£				£
19.. Jan 19	To Cash . .	3	45·74	19.. Jan 12	By Purchases Book	71	48·15
	Discount . .	3	2·41				
			48·15				48·15

Dr. STOCK **Cr.**

			£				
19.. Feb 1	To Balance . .		109·65				

Dr. TRADING ACCOUNT **Cr.**

			£				£
19.. Jan 31	To Purchases as per Purchases Book .	11	183·75	19.. Jan 31	By Sales, as per Sales Book .	14	88·93
					Stock on hand .		109·65
	Balance, trans- ferred to Profit & Loss . .	37	14·83				
			198·58				198·58

Dr. PROFIT AND LOSS ACCOUNT **Cr.**

			£				£
19.. Jan 30	To Cash (Rent) .	3	5·00	19.. Jan 31	By Discounts as per Cash Book .	5	8·57
	„ (Wages) .	3	9·78		Gross Profit from Trading Account .	37	14·83
31	Discounts as per Cash Book .	5	0·73				
	Transfer to Capital Ac- count (net gain) . .	35	7·89				
			23·40				23·40

QUESTIONS

1. How do you balance a person's account?

2. Which are the last accounts to be balanced?

3. What must you do before balancing the Trading Account?

4. How is the stock on hand ascertained in business?

5. Where do you transfer the balance of Trading Account?

6. Where do you transfer the balance of Profit and Loss Account?

EXERCISE ON CHAPTER IX

EXERCISE 26

From the following statement compile Cash Book, Purchases Book, Sales Book, and Ledger. Post the first three books into the Ledger, draw out a Trial Balance, and Profit and Loss Account. Value Goods on hand on 30th Jan., at £495·53.

19..		£
Jan 1	W. Beaty commenced business with cash . . .	700·00
2	Paid into Bank	600·00
4	Bought of Rayner & Co. Iron £350, Steel £180 .	530·00
6	Sold to Barker & Co. Iron £75, Steel £62·50 . .	137·50
8	Sold to K. Bentley Iron £38, Steel £13 . .	51·00
11	Received from Barker & Co.	75·00
12	Drew from Bank	400·00
13	Paid Rayner & Co. £503·50. Was allowed discount £26·50	530·00
14	Bought of Rayner & Co. Steel £100, Iron £70 . .	170·00
19	Received from K. Bentley £49·73. Allowed him discount £1·27	51·00
21	Sold to Barker & Co. Steel £20, Iron £10 . .	30·00
24	Bought of Mersey Iron Co. Iron £75 . . .	75·00
26	Sold to K. Bentley, Iron £50, Steel £5 . . .	55·00
27	Received cash for Ready Money Sales . . .	25·53
28	Paid into Bank	100·00
30	Paid Trade Expenses	15·38

CHAPTER X

THE BALANCE SHEET

WE have now completed our record of the month's transactions, posted and balanced the Ledger, and we can, therefore, duly present the result in the form of a **Balance Sheet,**
which is *a brief summary, showing the balances of accounts, and
whether we are solvent or insolvent.*

In this statement are presented the balances of all accounts
owing *by* us, which are called our *Liabilities*; it contains, also,
the balances of all accounts owing *to* us, and of property of
any kind *belonging to us*, which are called our *Assets.* When
our Assets exceed our Liabilities, we are said to be *Solvent*,
able to pay our debts; when our Liabilities exceed our Assets,
we are considered to be *Insolvent*, unable to pay our debts.

In the Balance Sheet the left-hand side is headed *Liabilities*,
and the right-hand side *Assets.* If we remember that Liabilities
are debts owing *by* us, and that Assets are debts owing *to* us,
we shall have no difficulty in going through the Ledger, and
placing the balances on their proper side in the Balance Sheet.
When this has been done the Balance Sheet will appear as
follows—

BALANCE SHEET OF E. KEANE, 31ST JANUARY, 19..

Liabilities				£	Assets					£
H. Harper	.	.	.	12·25	Cash in hand	.	.	.	.	20·74
Balance (Capital)	.	.	.	507·89	E. Cleaver	.	.	.	.	19·00
					G. Gray	.	.	.	.	9·25
					Bank	.	.	.	.	350·00
					W. Hope	.	.	.	.	11·50
					Goods (Stock on hand)			.	.	109·65
				520·14						520·14

If we compare the balance, as shown by the Balance Sheet,
with the balance of the Capital Account, we shall find that

they are exactly the same, as they ought to be, because our Capital is what we are *worth* after deducting our Liabilities from our Assets; in other words, it is the *excess* of our Assets over our Liabilities.

We have now completed our work for the month. We have tested our accuracy by the Trial Balance, balancing the Ledger, and by the Balance Sheet; and we have the satisfaction of pronouncing it *correct*

QUESTIONS

1 What is a Balance Sheet?

2. What do you mean by Solvent? What by Insolvent?

3 What are Liabilities? What are Assets?

4. On which side of the Balance Sheet do you enter Liabilities?

5. What does the balance of the Balance Sheet represent?

6 What do you mean by "Capital"?

It may be convenient to have the set of transactions which we have worked through, in a complete form, and it is accordingly given here—

19..			£
Jan 1	E. Keane commenced business with cash . . .		500·00
2	Paid into Bank		400·00
	Bought of H. Harper, Manchester,		
	20 yds. Black Cloth @ £1·75; 15 yds. Brown Cloth @ £1·25		53·75
3	Sold to E. Cleaver, Bolton,		
	4 yds. Black Cloth @ £2·13; 2 yds. Brown Cloth @ £1·18		10·88
4	Bought of C. Taylor, Rochdale,		
	5 pairs Blankets @ £6		30·00
6	Bought of A. Armstrong, Leeds,		
	1 doz. Shawls @ £2·43 each; 5 Shawls @ £2·09 .		39·61
8	Paid H. Harper,		
	Cash £51·06; and was allowed discount £2·69 .		53·75
9	Received from E. Cleaver,		
	Cash £10·60; allowed him discount £0·28 . .		10·88

19..		£
Jan 10	Sold to G. Gray, Oldham,	
	4 pairs Blankets @ £3·63; 3 Shawls @ £1·26 each	18·30
11	Paid C. Taylor,	
	Cash £28·50; was allowed discount £1·50 . .	30·00
12	Bought of T. Atkins, Manchester,	
	10 yds. Sheeting @ £1·25; 15 yds. Sheeting @ £1·88;	
	Trimmings for £7·45	48·15
13	Sold to W. Hope, Stockport,	
	3 pairs Blankets @ £3·00; 4 Shawls @ £2·64; 6 yds.	
	Black Cloth @ £1·99	31·50
18	Received from G. Gray,	
	Cash £17·84; allowed him discount £0·46 . .	18·30
	Paid A. Armstrong,	
	Cash £37·63; was allowed discount £1·98 . .	39·61
	Drew from Bank	60·00
19	Paid T. Atkins,	
	Cash £45·74; was allowed discount £2·41 . .	48·15
20	Paid into Bank	10·00
22	Received from W. Hope.	20·00
24	Bought of H. Harper,	
	25 yds. Black Cloth @ £0·49	12·25
26	Sold to E. Cleaver,	
	5 yds. Black Cloth @ £2·13; 3 yds. Velvet @ £2·38;	
	Trimmings £1·21	19·00
30	Sold to G. Gray,	
	2 yds. Black Cloth @ £2·00; 5 Shawls @ £1·05 .	9·25
	Paid Rent	5·00
	Paid Wages	9·78
	Stock of Goods unsold valued at £109·65	

EXERCISES ON CHAPTER X

Ex. 27. Make out Balance Sheet for Exercise 26 in Chapter IX.

Ex. 28. Make out Profit and Loss Account and Balance Sheet for Exercise 25 in Chapter VIII. Take the value of the stock as being £350.

CHAPTER XI

REVISION

BEFORE proceeding with the next stage of our study, let us review briefly what we have already learned about the subject.

We have seen that the *receiver* is always considered to be the *debtor*, while the *sender* or *payer* is always looked upon as the *creditor*; that there cannot be a debtor without a creditor, since a receiver implies also a giver; and that, therefore, every transaction has a double effect, namely, that every *debit* has a corresponding *credit*, the recording of which, in the Ledger, constitutes the *Double Entry* System of Book-keeping, as distinguished from *Single Entry*, where each transaction is recorded *once* only in the Ledger.

We have learned, too, that the Cash Book is the Cash Account bound up separately and that it contains the record of all our receipts and payments of cash, together with the amount of discount allowed by us to other persons or by them to us; that the Dr. side of the Cash Book is posted to the Cr. side of the Ledger, and the Cr. side of the Cash Book to the Dr. side of the Ledger; while the total amount of discount allowed to us, or by us, is transferred to the Profit and Loss Account, also in the Ledger.

We have seen, also, that our purchases on credit are recorded in the Purchases Book, and that the entries in this book are posted to the Cr. side of the Ledger, because the *senders* of the goods are our *creditors* for the value of the goods sent; and that, at the end of each month, the total of goods *received* is posted to the Dr. side of the Trading Account in the Ledger, because the receiver is debtor, and the Trading Account has received the goods during the month.

On the other hand, we have learned to record our *Sales* on credit in the Sales Book, and have seen that this book is posted to the Dr. side of the Ledger, because the persons who *received* the goods are our *debtors* for the value of the goods they received from us. Then we saw that, at the end of the month, the total amount of goods *sold* was transferred to the Cr. side of the Trading Account in the Ledger, because the sender is creditor, and the Trading Account *sent out* the goods during the month.

Then, to test the accuracy of our posting, we learned how to make out a Trial Balance; to see whether the total of the Dr. entries in the Ledger equalled the total of the Cr. entries, as should be the case if every *debit* has a corresponding *credit*. The Trial Balance completed, we saw how to balance our accounts in the Ledger, by finding the difference between the two sides of each account. But, with regard to the Trading Account, *before* balancing, we found it was necessary to put on the Cr. side our stock of goods *unsold*, since otherwise we could not say whether we had made a profit or sustained a loss. The balance of the Trading Account we transferred to the *opposite* side of Profit and Loss Account, because the balance represented always a gain or a loss. The difference between the two sides of the Profit and Loss Account was our *net* gain or loss, and this we transferred to the *opposite* side of Capital Account, because it either increased or decreased the amount of capital invested in the business.

Finally, we saw that the Balance Sheet was a brief statement of our affairs, showing our Assets and Liabilities, and that the *excess* of the amount of our Assets over what we owe to others constituted our *capital*, or what we were *worth*, and that, therefore, this amount should be the same as the balance of the Capital Account.

Our study, so far, has probably shown us the importance of method in the keeping of accounts, if our book-keeping is to fulfil its object and provide us with a ready means of ascertaining, at any time, the exact state of our business affairs. It has shown us, also, that all the entries are made on the principle that the receiving account is always debtor to the *sending* account.

Now we may go further, and we shall find that the principles we have already learned will help us very much in our future study.

QUESTIONS

1. Who is always considered as the Dr.?

2. What is Double Entry?

3. To which side of the Ledger do you post entries on the Dr. side of the Cash Book?

4. Where do you transfer the Discount entered in the Cash Book?

5. What is the Purchases Book, and to which side of the Ledger is it posted?

6. Explain the use of the Sales Book, and how it is posted to the Ledger.

7. What is a Trial Balance? A Balance Sheet?

8. Where do you transfer the balance of Profit and Loss? Why?

EXERCISE 29

Enter the following transactions, using Cash Book, Purchases Book, and Sales Book. Post to Ledger Accounts; make Trial Balance, Profit and Loss Account, and Balance Sheet.

		£
19..		
Sep 1	A. Graham commenced business with cash	750·00
3	Purchased Goods from A. Peters	250·00
4	,, ,, for cash	27·67
5	Sold Goods for cash	25·00
8	,, ,, to W. Trainer	50·00
9	,, ,, to R. Roberts	27·17
11	Purchased Goods from H. Morton	100·00
12	Paid A. Peters, cash	150·00
15	Received Cash from W. Trainer	30·00
18	,, ,, ,, R. Roberts	17·17
19	Bought Goods from A. Peters	50·00
23	Sold Goods to W. Trainer for cash	125·00
25	Sent Cash to A. Peters	100·00
26	Paid Wages	37·43
30	Remitted Cash to H. Morton	50·00

Goods on hand valued at £200·50.

CHAPTER XII

CASH BOOK WITH BANK COLUMN

WE saw on page 2 that a Bank was a place where a business man could put his spare cash and be sure that it was in safe keeping. If the amount was very large in proportion to his business, part might be left with the banker for a definite period, say, six months, the customer promising not to disturb the money during that time. The banker in return for the use of this money would allow the customer interest, that is the banker would pay an extra amount of money. Such a bank account would be called a "Deposit Account." The rest of the money would be put into the bank on the understanding that it could be added to or taken out when required. The bank account under this arrangement would be called a "Current Account." When a trader wishes to put money into his Current Account at a bank he fills in a slip of paper called a "Paying-in Slip," and when he wishes to take money out he makes out or "draws" a cheque. A **Cheque** is an order upon a particular banker to pay a certain specified sum of money to a person named, or to bearer.

Cheques are made payable to *bearer* or *to order*; and they are either *open* or *crossed* cheques. When drawn payable to *bearer*, the banker will pay the amount of the cheque to any person who presents it for payment. When drawn payable to *order*, the payee must sign his name on the back before the cheque will be honoured, unless it is paid into his account for collection. Such a signing is called *endorsing*. A *crossed* cheque has two parallel lines drawn across its face, with the words "& Co." between. Such a cheque cannot be cashed; that is to say, the banker will not pay *money* for it, but he will give the person paying it into the bank *credit* for the amount stated on the cheque. A cheque which is not crossed is called an *open* cheque.

The greater number of the payments in actual business are made by means of cheques. To save trouble in entering these, most book-keepers have a special column ruled on each side of the Cash Book, and the cheques received or paid are entered in these columns, in the same way as the discount allowed to or by them is entered in the discount column.

The additional column for the Bank is placed next to the cash column on each side of the Cash Book. The columns are headed respectively Discount, Office Cash, and Bank.

The Dr. side of the Cash Book, we may remind the student, is the *received* side; so that when either Cash or the Bank *receives* an amount, it is entered on the Dr. side of the Cash Book, in the Cash or Bank column, according to the account which receives the amount. On the other hand, the Cr. side of the Cash Book is the *paid* side; so that when either Cash or the Bank *pays* an amount, it is entered on the Cr. side, in the column for Office Cash or Bank, as the case may be.

When, therefore, we *receive* payment of an account, either in cash or by cheque, the amount is entered in the Cash or Bank column on the Dr. side, and the discount allowed by us, if any, is entered in the Discount column on the *same* side. When we *pay* an account in *cash*, it is entered in the Cash column on the Cr. side, and the discount allowed to us, if any, is entered in the Discount column on the *same* side. And when we *pay* an account by *cheque*, the amount is entered in the Bank column on the Cr. side, because it is, in reality, a payment by the Bank. This will easily be understood if we consider that the person to whom we pay the cheque will take it, or send it, to the Bank, and will then receive payment of the amount stated.

When we ourselves withdraw money from the Bank, however, it is, at the *same* time, both a *receipt* and a *payment*. It is a receipt by us, and it is a payment by the Bank; so that it requires an entry on *each* side of the Cash Book, namely, in the *Cash* column on the Dr. side, because the Cash *receives* it, and in the *Bank* column on the Cr. side, because the *Bank pays* it.

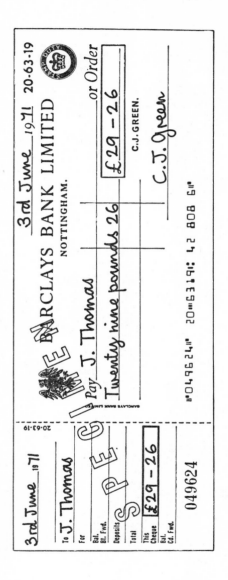

A Cheque

A RECEIPT

£10·60

Received *from* Mr. Ernest Cleaver, Bolton,

the sum of Ten pounds 60,

in payment of account rendered.

Edward Kleane.

STAMP

In the same way, when we pay money into the Bank, it is, at once, both a *payment* and a *receipt*. It is a payment by us and it is a receipt by the Bank; so that it requires *two* entries in the Cash Book, one in the Cash column on the Cr. side, because the Cash *pays* it, and another in the Bank column on the Dr. side, because the Bank *receives* it.

It is possible by using a Bank column in the Cash Book, to dispense with a Bank Account in the Ledger.

Such a Cash Book as we have just described is posted into the Ledger in the same way as the Cash Book we used in the first few chapters of this book; that is to say, the individual items in both the Cash and Bank columns on the debit side are posted to the credit side of the accounts in the Ledger and at the end of the month the total of the discount allowed by us, which will be the total of the Discount column on the Dr. side, is transferred to the Dr. side of Discount Account in the Ledger, or *direct* to Profit and Loss. On the other hand, the individual items on the credit side, in both columns, are posted to the debit side of the accounts in the Ledger and the total of the discount allowed to us, which will be the total of the Discount column on the Cr. side, is carried to the Cr. side of Discount Account in the Ledger, or *direct* to Profit and Loss. Thus it will be seen that when a cheque is *received*, we *debit* the Bank, and *credit* the *sender* of the cheque; when a cheque is *paid* away, we *debit* the *receiver* of the cheque, and *credit* the Bank. In other words, we act on the principle we have followed all along of debiting the receiving account and crediting the sending account.

Suppose the Cash and Bank transactions for a month to be as follows—

19..			£
Jan 1	Cash in hand	. . . . . .	70·50
	Cash in Bank	. . . . .	3,500·00
2	Paid A. Beale by cash	. . . .	47·50
	And was allowed discount	. . .	2·50
3	Paid Smith & Co. by cheque	. . .	500·00
5	Received cheque from S. Gordon	. . .	19·00
	And allowed him discount	. . .	1·00
8	Received Cash for Goods sold	. . .	45·78

Dr. CASH

Date	Receipts	L.F.	Discount	Office Cash	Bank
19..			£	£	£
Jan 1	To Balance	b/d		70·50	3,500·00
5	S. Gordon		1·00	45·78	19·00
8	Sales				
10	Cash			25·00	60·00
15	Bank				95·50
28	Sales				
			1·00	141·28	3,674·50
Feb 1	To Balance	b/d		17·95	3,047·12

CONTRA **Cr.**

Date	Payments	L.F.	Discount	Office Cash	Bank
19..			£	£	£
Jan 1	By A. Beale		2·50	47·50	
3	Smith & Co			60·00	500·00
10	Bank				25·00
15	Office Cash				18·50
18	P. & L. (Water Rate)			15·83	
22	Purchases				62·00
29	H. Simpson				21·88
31	P. & L. (Trade Expenses)				3,047·12
	Balance	c/d		17·95	
			2·50	141·28	3,674·50

						£
19..						
Jan 10	Paid into Bank .	.	.	.	.	60·00
15	Drew cheque for Office Cash	.	.	.	.	25·00
18	Paid Water Rate by cheque	.	.	.	.	18·50
22	Bought Goods and paid for same by cash	.	.	.	.	15·83
28	Sold Goods and received cheque for same	.	.	.	.	95·50
29	Sent cheque to H. Simpson .	.	.	.	.	62·00
31	Paid Trade Expenses by cheque .	.	.	.	.	21·88

The Cash Book entered up as explained, would appear as shown opposite.

Note. The *balances in hand* at the beginning of the month are not posted as receipts for the month. They cannot, of course, be reckoned as such, since they are the balances from *preceding* months, and to include them again would be to debit the Cash and Bank *twice* with the same amount.

It is an unfortunate fact that sometimes after a cheque has been paid into the Bank it is returned to us marked R/D (refer to drawer) or N/F (no funds). This means that our customer cannot pay or "*honour*" his cheque, which is thus said to be "*dishonoured*." Since the Bank have returned the cheque, we must make an entry in our Cash Book *crediting* the Bank column, and as our customer still owes us the amount, we *debit* his account.

The entries will appear as follows—

Cr.   CASH BOOK *(Contra)*

Date			Discount	Office	Bank
					£
	By Customer's A/c. (Cheque dis- honoured)				20·00

Dr.   CUSTOMER'S ACCOUNT   *Cr.*

		£	
To Cheque Dishonoured	.	20·00	

QUESTIONS

1. If you received payment by cheque, in which column, and on which side of the Cash Book, would you enter the amount?

2. What is a cheque? A *crossed* cheque? An *open* cheque?

3. Suppose you receive payment of an account in Cash, and you allow discount, how would you treat the transaction?

4. Will the banker pay you cash for a crossed cheque?

5. How would you enter a payment by cheque?

6. How would you treat a withdrawal of Cash from the Bank?

7. When a cheque is drawn payable to *order* what must be done before the banker will cash it?

8. What does *endorsing* a cheque mean?

EXERCISES ON CHAPTER XII

EXERCISE 30

From the following particulars, compile Cash Book with columns for Discount, Cash, and Bank—

19..		£
Feb 1	Cash in hand	90·50
	Cash in Bank	300·00
3	Paid to G. Ovens, cheque	35·53
5	Received Cash from B. Abel	66·50
	Allowed him discount	3·50
6	Paid into Bank	70·00
10	Paid A. Sibble, by cash	12·60
15	Received from W. Grafton, cheque	39·00
	Allowed him discount	1·00
18	Withdrew from Bank	60·00
	Bought Goods for cash	65·50
25	Sold Goods for cash	56·98
	Paid into Bank	56·98
28	Paid Trade Expenses by cheque	10·76

EXERCISE 31

From the following statement compile a Cash Book with columns for Discount, Cash, and Bank. Balance the Cash and Bank Accounts, and show total discount received and allowed.

		£
19..		
Mar 1	Cash at Office	139·53
	Cash at Bank	1,325·75
3	Paid J. Keeley by cash	9·50
	Was allowed discount	0·50
5	Received Cash for Goods sold	95·83
	Received Cash from A. Moss	27·85
	Paid into Bank	120·00
8	Bought Goods for cash	26·53
10	Drew cheque for Office Cash	20·00
16	Bought additional Office Furniture (Debit Furniture	
	A/c), cheque	95·00
17	Bought Goods for cheque	148·53
24	Sold Goods for cash	250·00
	Paid into Bank	250·00
28	Paid B. Wright, cheque	97·50
	Was allowed discount	2·50
30	Bought Goods for Cash, giving cheque for . .	65·00
31	Paid Trade Expenses by cash	11·52

EXERCISE 32

Enter in the proper subsidiary books, post, and balance, drawing out Trial Balance, Profit and Loss Account, and Balance Sheet. Estimate Goods unsold at £410·53.

		£
19..		
Jan 1	Commenced Business with cash	2,000·00
2	Paid into Bank	1,950·00
4	Bought of Leeming Bros., Goods	500·00
5	Bought Goods of H. Lynes	100·00
8	Sold to Dempsey & Son, Goods	110·00
11	Paid Leeming Bros., by cheque	475·00
	Was allowed discount	25·00
12	Bought Goods of H. Lynes	153·50
13	Bought of Marsh & Co., Goods	180·50
15	Received of Dempsey & Son, cheque . . .	107·25
	Allowed discount	2·75
17	Sold to T. Raines, Goods	253·50
18	Sold to W. Knight, Goods	260·00
20	W. Knight sent cheque	253·50
	Allowed him discount	6·50
22	Received cash from T. Raines	250·98
	Allowed discount	2·52
	Paid into Bank	270·00
24	Paid Marsh & Co. by cheque	171·48
	Was allowed discount	9·02
27	Bought of Marsh & Co., Goods	85·75
31	Paid Trade Expenses by cheque	21·44

EXERCISE 33

Treat in the same way as No. 32. Value of Goods on hand at end of month, £194.

19..		£
Feb 1	Commenced Business with cash	1,000·00
2	Paid into Bank	950·00
4	Bought of Hood Bros., Goods	300·00
6	Sold to Winton & Sons, Goods	200·50
11	Paid Hood Bros., by cheque	200·00
13	Received from Winton & Sons, by cheque . .	100·00
18	Sold to G. Moody, Goods	50·00
20	Bought of Hannon & Co., Goods	250·50
22	Sent cheque to Hannon & Co.	242·98
	Was allowed discount	7·52
24	Sold Goods for cash	12·66
24	Sold Goods to Ashton & Sons	100·00
26	Received of Winton & Sons by cheque . . .	50·00
26	Received from G. Moody by cheque . . .	48·75
	Allowed him discount	1·25
27	Bought of E. Fowler, Goods.	117·53
27	Bought Goods for cash	15·00
28	Sold to H. Cowburn, Goods	180·50
28	Trade Expenses, paid by cash	22·75

CHAPTER XIII

CASH BOOK (contd.)

BANK BALANCE RECONCILIATION, ETC.

IT can be seen from the bank column of the Cash Book on page 50 that there is a balance of £3,047·12. But the question arises: What evidence have we that there is actually that balance in our bank account?

We have already mentioned the Paying-in Slip, showing the Banker what amount is paid in, and the cheque showing what is drawn out; from these two sources of information is compiled our account in the Banker's Ledger. A copy of this account is supplied to us in the form of a Bank Statement, from which we can check the items and see whether the balance does agree with our Cash Book. Usually it will not. For instance, on our Bank Statement we find that the balance on 31st Jan. is £3,035·50. It is, therefore, necessary to check each individual item on the Bank Statement with the bank column of our Cash Book. When this has been done we find that the item of £95·50 was not entered on the Bank Statement until 1st Feb. Also, two items on the credit side of the Cash Book, viz. £62 and £21·88, did not appear on the Bank Statement, showing that these cheques had not been presented to our Bank for payment. Having found how the difference arises we must prepare a statement, known as a Bank Reconciliation Statement, in the following manner—

BANK RECONCILIATION STATEMENT AT 31ST JANUARY

			£
Balance as Bank Statement	.	.	3,035·50
Less Unpresented Cheques	.	.	83·88
			2,951·62
Add Cheques not credited	.	.	95·50
Balance as Cash Book	.	.	3,047·12

PETTY CASH BOOK

It very often happens that many of the Expenses incurred in a business are of small amounts. Therefore, in order to prevent the Cash Book being overloaded with numerous unimportant items, a subsidiary book, called **Petty Cash Book**, is used. A simple form of Petty Cash Book contains a total column and other columns for different items of expenditure such as Postage, Travelling, Carriage, and General Expenses.

A more advanced method is used when a stated sum of money is given every week or month by the Chief Cashier of a business to a Junior Clerk for the purpose of making these small payments. At the end of the period an amount equal to the expenses is handed to the Petty Cashier, thus making up the balance to the stated amount. This method is known as the "Imprest" system.

Let us take an example—

```
19..
Jan  1    Chief Cashier advanced to Petty Cashier, £5.
     2    Paid Bus Fares, 5p; Stamps, 28p.
     3     ,,   Train Fares, 13p;  Parcel Post, 9p.
     4     ,,   for Cleaning Offices, £1·25.
     5     ,,    ,,  Typewriting Carbons, 93p.
     6     ,,    ,,  Printed Letter Paper, £1·13.
```

Dr.   *Cr.*

Cash Recd.	Date		Total	Travelling	Postage	Stationery	Cleaning
£ 5·00	19.. Jan 1	To Cash	£	£	£	£	£
	2	By Fares	0·05	0·05			
		Stamps	0·28		0·28		
	3	Train Fares	0·13	0·13			
		Parcel Post	0·09		0·09		
	4	Office Cleaning	1·25				1·25
	5	Typewriting Carbons	0·93			0·39	
	6	Letter Paper	1·13			1·13	
			3·86	0·18	0·37	2·06	1·25
	8	To Cash	*1·14*				
		By Balance	*5·00*				
5·00 *8·86*			*5·00* *8·86*				
1·14 *5·00*	19.. Jan 9	To Balance b/d					
3·86		*Cash*					

Exercises on Chapter XIII
EXERCISE 34

The balance of T. Hull's Cash Book on 30th June was £539·06, but his Bank Statement showed a balance of £289·77. On comparing his Bank Statement with his Cash Book, it was found that cheques £98·01, £208·82 and £84·74 had been paid in, but not entered on the Bank Statement, while two cheques for £41·04 and £101·23 had been drawn but not presented. Prepare the Reconciliation Statement.

EXERCISE 35

F. Smith's Cash Book showed a balance of cash at Bank of £327·95 on 31st December. His Bank Statement showed an overdraft of £267·89 on that date. The difference arose as follows—

A cheque for £32·94 drawn by F. Smith, had not been presented for payment; £616·45 received on 31st December was not credited by the Bank until 1st January; the Bank had charged him with £12·33 Interest which was not entered in the Cash Book. Prepare the Reconciliation Statement. (R.S.A.)

EXERCISE 36

F. Holmes allowed his Petty Cashier £10 on the Imprest System on 1st June. During that month he had the following expenses—

19..		£
Jun 1	Balance in hand	10·00
2	Paid for Stationery, £2·46, and Stamps, 50p	2·96
3	Paid Travelling Expenses, 23p; Parcels, 10p	0·33
5	Bought N.H. & U.I. Stamps	0·81
6	Paid for Tea and Biscuits	0·13
8	Bought Blotting Paper	0·75
9	Paid for String, 12p; Cleaning Windows, 30p.	0·42
10	Paid for Stamps	0·35
11	Paid for Bus Fares, 8p; Telegram, 11p	0·19
12	Bought N.H. & U.I. Stamps	0·81
13	Paid for Tea and Biscuits	0·13

Enter these expenses in a Columnar Petty Cash Book, balance it, and draw a cheque for the Imprest on 13th June.

CHAPTER XIV

RETURNS BOOKS

In almost every business it is the rule rather than the exception that some goods have for various reasons to be returned to the seller. For example, the goods may be of wrong quality, or a portion of the invoice was not ordered; but whatever the reason, we must make entries in our books for these goods which we return. In the first instance, a letter is sent complaining of the goods, and if the seller is agreeable the goods are returned. As each return occurs, we enter the date, to whom sent, particulars of the goods, reason for return, and the amount, in a **Returns Outwards Book.** Alternatively, the particulars of the goods and the reason column may be omitted, and then the ruling would be the same as the Purchases Book on page 11.

With the goods is sometimes sent a **Debit Note** giving full particulars of the goods and reason for their return. In any event, the seller, if he agrees to the reason for the return, will send a **Credit Note** showing that in his Ledger the customer's account has been credited.

Let us take an example—

Jan 10. Returned to D. Wilson, 2 doz. tins of fruit damaged, £0·60.

RETURNS OUTWARDS BOOK

Date	Particulars	Led. Fol.	£
19.. Jan 10	D. Wilson		0·60

Since D. Wilson has received these goods, we must *debit* his account, and consequently our Purchases Account must be *credited.* The accounts will then appear as follows.

Dr.   D. WILSON   *Cr.*

		£
19.. Jan 10	To Goods . .	0·60

Dr.   PURCHASES ACCOUNT   *Cr.*

		£
19.. Jan 10	By Returns . .	0·60

As *we* return goods to the sellers, so, on the other hand, are goods returned to us by our customers, i.e. they are **Returns Inwards.** Since we receive the goods, Sales Account will be *debited* and the customer's account will be *credited*.

EXERCISES ON CHAPTER XIV
EXERCISE 37

On 1st July C. Jeffrey commenced business with Cash at Bank £1,000. His transactions for July were as follows. Enter them in the Cash Book, Purchases, Sales and Returns Books. Make a Trial Balance, Profit and Loss Account, and Balance Sheet.

19.. Jul		£
2	Advanced to Office Cash	25·00
	Bought Goods from A. Mitchell	200·00
4	,, ,, ,, J. Thomson	100·00
	Sold Goods to F. Winsor	75·00
5	Paid cheque to A. Mitchell	100·00
6	Cash Sales for week	18·00
8	Returned Goods to J. Thomson	10·00
10	Sold Goods to B. Fields	50·00
12	Sent cheque to A. Mitchell	100·00
13	Cash Sales for week	20·00
15	Sold Goods to G. Saville	63·00
16	Sent cheque to J. Thomson, £50	50·00
17	Received cheque from F. Winsor, £45 . . .	45·00
	G. Saville returned Goods	3·00
18	Sold Goods to F. Winsor	55·00
	Sent cheque to J. Thomson	40·00
19	Received cheque from B. Fields	50·00
20	Trade Expenses paid in cash	10·00
	Cash Sales	23·00
	Stock on hand	100·00

EXERCISE 38

On 1st March J. Matlock commenced business with Cash
£3,500 which was paid into Bank. Enter the transactions for
March in the Cash Book, Purchases, Sales, and Returns
Books. Make a Trial Balance, Profit and Loss Account, and
Balance Sheet.

19..		£
Mar 1	Bought Goods from C. Cray	400·00
3	Sold Goods to T. Manton	150·00
4	Sold Goods for cash	37·00
6	Paid C. Cray by cheque	100·00
	T. Manton returned Goods	20·00
8	Sold Goods to H. Cleaver	175·00
10	Bought Goods from A. Merrall	110·00
12	Received cheque from T. Manton	70·00
	Sold Goods for cash	31·00
13	Paid various Expenses by cash	12·00
	Returned Goods to A. Merrall	10·00
15	Paid C. Cray, by cheque	100·00
	Sold Goods to J. Timson	55·00
17	Received cheque from T. Manton	60·00
19	Sent A. Merrall cheque	60·00
20	Cash Sales for week	43·00
22	Received cheque from H. Cleaver	75·00
	Bought Goods from A. Merrall	130·00
24	Paid C. Cray, by cheque	100·00
26	Bought Goods for cheque	52·00
27	Paid various Expenses in cash	11·00
	Paid into Bank	75·00
	Stock on hand	280·00

CHAPTER XV

THE JOURNAL

WE have now a knowledge of five subsidiary books, namely, Cash Book, Purchases Book, Sales Book, Returns Outwards and Returns Inwards Books. In most businesses, however, there are transactions which would not properly fall under any one of these heads, and a further subsidiary book, therefore, becomes necessary, in order to prepare the entries of these transactions for the Ledger. The **Journal** is such a book.

The *business* use of the Journal is to record transactions for which there are no special books provided, such as transactions involving interest, commissions, etc.; its *theoretical* use is to show more clearly the principles of Book-keeping by Double Entry, as, by means of this book, the student is enabled to see at once the double effect of each transaction, namely, that every *debit* has a corresponding *credit*. It is in this latter way that we shall use the Journal in the next few pages. When this course is adopted, it is not necessary to use the Cash Book, Purchases Book, etc., because all entries are passed through the Journal, and posted from it to the Ledger.

EXERCISE 39

WASTE BOOK

19..		£
Jan 2	Commenced Business with cash	1,000·00
4	Bought Goods for cash	500·00
5	Sold Goods for cash	100·00
6	Bought of W. Bell, Goods	250·50
10	Sold Goods to A. Weld	50·00
12	Paid W. Bell £244·24; was allowed discount £6·26	250·50
14	Bought of H. Keeling, Goods	70·00
16	Received from A. Weld, Cash, £47·50; allowed discount £2·50	50·00
17	Sold Goods to E. Thomas	85·75
20	,, ,, A. Weld	40·53
24	,, ,, for cash	25·00
31	Paid Trade Expenses	13·28

The statement of the transactions which are to be journalized (entered in the Journal) is made in what is called the Waste Book.

The Journal is ruled just as we ruled our Trial Balance paper, but with the addition of a column for the date.

JOURNAL FOR EXERCISE 39

19..				Dr. £	Cr. £
Jan 2	Cash . . .	Dr.		1,000·00	
	To Capital . . .				1,000·00
4	Purchases . . .	Dr.		500·00	
	To Cash . . .				500·00
5	Cash . . .	Dr.		100·00	
	To Sales . . .				100·00
6	Purchases . . .	Dr.		250·50	
	To W. Bell . . .				250·50
10	A. Weld . . .	Dr.		50·00	
	To Sales . . .				50·00
12	W. Bell . . .	Dr.		250·50	
	To Cash . . .				244·24
	Profit and Loss (Discount)				6·26
14	Purchases . . .	Dr.		70·00	
	To H. Keeling . . .				70·00
16	Cash . . .	Dr.		47·50	
	Profit and Loss (Discount)	Dr.		2·50	
	To A. Weld . . .				50·00
17	E. Thomas . . .	Dr.		85·75	
	To Sales . . .				85·75
20	A. Weld . . .	Dr.		40·53	
	To Sales . . .				40·53
24	Cash . . .	Dr.		25·00	
	To Sales . . .				25·00
31	Profit and Loss (Trade Expen.) . .	Dr.		13·28	
	To Cash . . .				13·28
	Total .			2,435·56	2,435·56

We saw very early in our study of the subject that the *receiver* is always the *debtor*, while the *sender* is always *creditor* by (for) what he sent. In journalizing, we *state* these facts in every transaction, as will be seen from the specimen Journal given above.

NOTES ON THE JOURNAL FOR EXERCISE 39

The *Debit* entry is always made *first*.

19..

Jan 2   Cash Account *receives* and is, therefore, *Debtor*; Capital (the owner of the business) *gives* and is, therefore, *Creditor*.

4   Purchases Account *receives* and, so, is *Dr.*; Cash *sends* the Goods, or causes them to be sent, and is, therefore, *Cr.*

5
24   Cash *receives* and is *Dr.*; Sales Account *sends* the cash, or causes it to be sent, and is *Cr.*

6
14   Purchases Account *receives* and is *Dr.*; W. Bell and H. Keeling *send* the goods and are *Crs.*

10
17   A. Weld and E. Thomas *receive* the goods and are, accordingly,
20   *Drs.*; the Sales Account *sends* and, so, is *Cr.*

12   W. Bell *receives* the cash and a *loss* (by allowing discount) and, so, is *Dr.* for the cash *and* the amount of discount he allowed; the Cash Account *sends* or pays the amount, £244·24, and is *Cr.* for this sum; the Profit and Loss Account is *credited* with gains, and, as discount allowed to us is a *gain*, the Profit and Loss is *Cr.* for the discount, £6·26.

16   Cash *receives* £47·50 and is *Dr.* for this amount; Profit and Loss Account is *debited* with *losses*, and, as discount allowed by us is a *loss,* the Profit and Loss Account is *Dr.* for the discount, £2·50. Since A. Weld *sends* the cash and is *allowed* the discount, he is *Cr.* for the total amount, £50.

31   Trade Expense is a *loss*, since it reduces our profits on the business, and Profit and Loss Account is, therefore, *Dr.* for the amount, while Cash is *Cr.* because it *pays* it.

The rule is: *debit* the *receiving account*, and *credit* the *sending account*.

QUESTIONS

1   What is the business use of the Journal?

2. What is its theoretical use?

3. What other book is rendered necessary by using the Journal?

4. What is the rule in journalizing?

5. Which account is debited with losses?

EXERCISES ON CHAPTER XV
EXERCISE 40

Journalize the following transactions—

19..		£
Feb 1	Commenced Business with cash	300·00
4	Bought of T. Hales, Goods	50·53
8	Sold to D. Deakin, Goods	10·25
12	Sold Goods for cash	15·26
15	Paid T. Hales, cash	50·53
22	Bought Goods for cash	20·00
28	Paid Trade Expenses	4·26

From the Waste Book, draw up a Journal—

EXERCISE 41

19..		£
Jul 1	Commenced Business with cash	1,000·00
2	Bought Goods for cash	600·00
4	Sold Goods for cash	150·53
7	Bought of A. White, Goods	200·00
10	Sold to B. Black, Goods	60·50
14	Paid A. White on account (*towards* the £200 I owe)	150·00
20	Received of B. Black on account (*towards* the £60·50 he owes)	40·50
24	Bought Goods for cash	50·00
26	Sold Goods for cash	185·75
31	Paid Trade Expenses, cash	15·48

EXERCISE 42

19..		£
Aug 1	Commenced Business with cash	500·00
2	Bought Goods for cash	150·50
4	Sold Goods for cash	20·28
8	Bought Goods of A. Neale	80·50
10	Sold Goods to B. Edwards	25·18
15	Paid A. Neale, cash	80·50
18	Received from B. Edwards, cash	25·18
22	Sold Goods to R. Cattell	15·25
24	Bought Goods of G. Hanley.	50·50
31	Paid Trade Expenses	8·87

CHAPTER XVI

POSTING THE JOURNAL

IN posting the entries from the Journal to the Ledger, the items are taken direct to the accounts named, in the order in which they are stated in the Journal. For example, in the Journal for Exercise 39, the first entry would be posted *first* to the Dr. side of Cash Account in the Ledger, and *then* to the Cr. side of Capital Account. And in like manner with all the other items, so that there will be *two* entries, a *debit* and a *credit*, for each transaction recorded in the Journal.

Now, post the Journal for Exercise 39 into the Ledger, make out a Trial Balance, balance and close the accounts, and prepare a Balance Sheet. Estimate the goods unsold at £549·53. When you have completed the work, compare the result with the following key—

LEDGER

Dr. CASH ACCOUNT *Cr.*

19..			£	19..			£
Jan 2	To Capital	. .	1,000·00	Jan 4	By Purchases . .		500·00
5	Sales	. .	100·00	12	W. Bell . .		244·24
16	A. Weld	. .	47·50	31	Profit & Loss		
24	Sales	. .	25·00		(Trade Expenses)		13·28
				31	Balance . c/d		414·98
			1,172·50				1,172·50
Feb 1	To Balance .	b/d	414·98				

Dr. CAPITAL ACCOUNT *Cr.*

19..			£	19..			£
Jan 31	To Balance .	c/d	1,020·79	Jan 2	By Cash . . .		1,000·00
				31	Transfer from Profit & Loss .		20·79
			1,020·79				1,020·79
				Feb 1	By Balance .	b/d	1,020·79

Dr.   A. WELD   *Cr.*

19..			£	19..			£
Jan 10	To Sales	. .	50·00	Jan 16	By Cash .	.	47·50
20	,,	. .	40·53		Discount	.	2·50
				31	Balance .	c/d	40·53
			90·53				90·53
Feb 1	To Balance .	b/d	40·53				

Dr.   H. KEELING   *Cr.*

19..			£	19..			£
Jan 31	To Balance .	c/d	70·00	Jan 14	By Purchases .	.	70·00
				Feb 1	By Balance .	b/d	70·00

Dr.   E. THOMAS   *Cr.*

19..			£	19..			£
Jan 17	To Sales	. .	85·75	Jan 31	By Balance .	c/d	85·75
Feb 1	To Balance .	b/d	85·75				

Dr.   W. BELL   *Cr.*

19..			£	19..			£
Jan 12	To Cash .	.	244·24	Jan 6	By Purchases .	.	250·50
	Discount .	.	6·26				
			250·50				250·50

Dr.   PURCHASES   *Cr.*

19..			£	19..		£
Jan 4	To Cash .	.	500·00	Jan 31	By Trading Account .	820·50
6	W. Bell .	.	250·50			
14	H. Keeling .	.	70·00			
			820·50			820·50

Dr.   SALES   *Cr.*

19..		£	19..			£
Jan 31	To Trading Account	301·28	Jan 5	By Cash .	.	100·00
			10	A. Weld .	.	50·00
			17	E. Thomas .	.	85·75
			20	A. Weld .	.	40·53
			24	Cash .	.	25·00
		301·28				301·28

Dr. STOCK *Cr.*

19..		£	
Feb 1	To Balance	549·53	

Dr. TRADING ACCOUNT *Cr.*

19..		£	19..		£
Jan 31	To Purchases	820·50	Jan 31	By Sales	301·28
	Profit & Loss Account	30·31		Stock at close	549·53
		850·81			850·81

Dr. PROFIT AND LOSS ACCOUNT *Cr.*

19..		£	19..		£
Jan 16	To A. Weld (Discount)	2·50	Jan 12	By W. Bell (Discount)	6·26
31	Cash (Trade Expenses)	13·28	31	Transfer from Trading	30·31
	Balance transferred to Capital	20·79			
		36·57			36·57

TRIAL BALANCE

	Dr.	*Cr.*
	£	£
Cash Account	414·98	
Capital Account		1,000·00
Purchases	820·50	
Sales		301·28
A. Weld	40·53	
Profit and Loss	9·52	
H. Keeling		70·00
E. Thomas	85·75	
	1,371·28	1,371·28

BALANCE SHEET, 31ST JANUARY, 19..

Liabilities		£	*Assets*		£
H. Keeling		70·00	Cash		414·98
Balance (Capital)		1,020·79	Goods		549·53
			A. Weld		40·53
			E. Thomas		85·75
		1,090·79			1,090·79

EXERCISE 43

Journalize, post, and balance the following transactions. Draw out a Trial Balance, Profit and Loss Account, and Balance Sheet—

19..		£
Mar 1	Commenced Business with cash	500·00
3	Bought Goods for cash	200·00
5	Sold to A. Dewse, Goods	75·50
8	Bought of B. Bray, Goods	55·23
10	Received from A. Dewse, cash . . .	50·00
14	Sold to A. Cottrell, Goods	40·50
17	Paid B. Bray, cash	52·46
	Was allowed discount	2·77
19	Sold Goods for cash	10·38
21	Bought of B. Bray, Goods	30·50
24	Received from A. Cottrell, cash . . .	38·48
	Allowed him discount	2·02
31	Paid Trade Expenses	7·46
	Value of Goods unsold (for Ledger only) £175.	

QUESTIONS

1. State the Journal entry for the following—

Sold Goods to H. Kay; Received Cash from W. Lee; Paid Cash for Trade Expenses; Paid Cash into Bank; Drew Cash from Bank.

2. What are assets? What are liabilities?

3. Why is discount posted to Profit and Loss?

4. Which side of Profit and Loss Account represents the gains?

EXERCISES ON CHAPTER XVI
EXERCISE 44

Journalize, post, and balance the following. Draw out a Trial Balance, Profit and Loss Account, and Balance Sheet. Value Stock of Goods on 30th Sept. at £257.

19..		£
Sep 1	Commenced Business with cash . . .	400·00
2	Bought Goods and paid for same in cash . .	300·00
4	Sold Goods to W. Hoy	120·00

19..							£
Sep 6	Sold Goods to D. Evans	.	.	.	.	.	40·50
10	Sold Goods for cash .	.	.	.	.	.	12·60
14	Bought Goods from F. Drake .	.	.	.	.	.	90·75
16	Received from D. Evans.	.	.	.	.	.	39·49
	Allowed him discount .	.	.	.	.	.	1·01
	Received from W. Hoy .	.	.	.	.	.	100·00
21	Paid F. Drake . .	.	.	.	.	.	86·21
	Was allowed discount .	.	.	.	.	.	4·54
26	Bought Goods of F. Drake	.	.	.	.	.	30·50
	Sold Goods to H. Berry .	.	.	.	.	.	10·53
30	Paid Trade Expenses .	.	.	.	.	.	9·26

EXERCISE 45

Journalize, post, and balance as before Stock on hand on 31st Oct. is £135·75.

19..							£
Oct 1	Commenced Business with cash	.	.	.	.	.	300·00
	Bought Goods for cash .	.	.	.	.	.	100·00
3	Sold Goods for cash .	.	.	.	.	.	40·50
8	Bought Goods from C. Done .	.	.	.	.	.	80·50
12	Sold Goods to W. Neale	.	.	.	.	.	30·75
15	Paid C. Done . .	.	.	.	.	.	76·48
	Was allowed discount .	.	.	.	.	.	4·02
18	Received from W. Neale	.	.	.	.	.	29·98
	Allowed him discount .	.	.	.	.	.	0·77
22	Sold Goods to W. Neale	.	.	.	.	.	5·00
	Sold Goods to N. Owen	.	.	.	.	.	12·00
26	Bought Goods of C. Done	.	.	.	.	.	28·50
31	Paid Trade Expenses .	.	.	.	.	.	6·78

CHAPTER XVII

OPENING THE BOOKS

WHEN we have presented to us the Balance Sheet of a firm that has been trading previously, and we open new accounts for the persons or accounts mentioned in the Balance Sheet, we are said to have "opened the books."

In making the first Journal entries from a Balance Sheet, or from a statement of affairs, the rule is to *debit the Assets*, and *credit the Liabilities*. Assets, as already explained, are debts owing *to* a firm; Liabilities are debts owing *by* a firm. The amount by which the Assets exceed the Liabilities is the *Capital*, or actual worth of the person or firm. If the opening Journal entries from the following Balance Sheet be carefully noticed, the method will be easily understood.

BALANCE SHEET OF CHARLES PEARSON, 1ST JANUARY, 19..

Liabilities	£	Assets	£
W. Yates	50·00	Cash in hand	50·00
H. Noble . : .	45·53	Cash in Bank	500·00
Balance (Capital) . : .	1,225·97	Goods on hand . . .	600·00
		W. Moss	80·50
		A. Norton . . .	30·75
		S. Smith	60·25
	1,321·50		1,321·50

JOURNAL		Dr.	Cr.
19..		£	£
Jan 1	Cash . . . . C.B. 70	50·00	
	Bank . . . . C.B. 70	500·00	
	Stock . . . L. 71	600·00	
	W. Moss . . . L. 71	80·50	
	A. Norton . . . L. 71	30·75	
	S. Smith . . . L. 71	60·25	
	To W. Yates . . L. 71		50·00
	H. Noble . . L. 71		45·53
	C. Pearson (Cap. A/c.). L. 71		1,225·97
		1,321·50	1,321·50

If the transactions for the month are given, as they would be in an examination paper, those that required journalizing, such as interest, commission, would be entered in the ordinary way, the first transaction being entered immediately under the total of the opening Journal entries.

In posting the *opening entries* into the Ledger, the words, "To Sundries," or "By Sundries," would be used, and for this reason: Charles Pearson has Cash in Hand, Cash in the Bank, and Goods in his Warehouse, belonging to him; he has also debts owing *to* him by W. Moss, A. Norton, and S. Smith. But, on the other hand, *he* owes money (probably for the Goods) to W. Yates and to H. Noble. It will be seen, therefore, that strictly speaking, *all* the assets do not belong to Charles Pearson, since there is something owing to Yates and to Noble. In other words, the assets are *partly debtor* to Yates and to Noble. Further, C. Pearson's Capital (what he is *worth*) is made up of *sundry* or several things, namely, Cash, Goods, and *Debts* which he expects will be paid in due time.

Now, instead of putting down the *names* of all the accounts which go to make up Charles Pearson's *Capital*, we put down in his account the words "By Sundries," *sundries* meaning *several* accounts. And, in the same way, instead of trying to explain in Yates's account, and in Noble's account, how their balances are made up, we say that they are creditors "By Sundries."

Where the entry is on the Dr. side, we use the phrase "To Sundries" for similar reasons. The opening entries in the specimen Journal, just given, when posted, would appear as follows—

Dr. CASH BOOK

Date	Receipts		Discount	Office	Bank
19.. Jan 1	To Balances	J. 69		£ 50·00	£ 500·00

Dr.			STOCK ACCOUNT				Cr.
19.. Jan 1	To Sundries	J. 69	£ 600·00				

Dr.			W. MOSS				Cr.
19.. Jan 1	To Sundries	J. 69	£ 80·50				

Dr.			A. NORTON				Cr.
19.. Jan 1	To Sundries	J. 69	£ 30·75				

Dr.			S. SMITH				Cr.
19.. Jan 1	To Sundries	J. 69	£ 60·25				

Dr.			W. YATES				Cr.
				19.. Jan 1	By Sundries .	J. 69	£ 50·00

Dr.			H. NOBLE				Cr.
				19.. Jan 1	By Sundries .	J. 69	£ 45·53

Dr.			CAPITAL ACCOUNT				Cr.
				19.. Jan 1	By Sundries .	J. 69	£ 1,225·97

EXERCISE 46

The following is the Balance Sheet of Francis Webb. From this you are required to open his books through the Journal, and, afterwards, to enter the transactions for March in the C.B., P.B., and S.B., post and balance the accounts, make out Trial Balance and Balance Sheet—

BALANCE SHEET OF FRANCIS WEBB, 28TH FEBRUARY, 19..

Liabilities		£	Assets		£
E. Wroe		25·50	Cash in hand		28·48
D. Done		10·53	Cash in Bank		960·53
Balance (Capital) . . .		1,511·92	Goofs on hand . . .		450·00
			A. Wade		45·28
			B. Brown		63·66
		1,547·95			1,547·95

TRANSACTIONS FOR MARCH

19..		£
Mar 1	Bought Goods and paid for same by cheque . .	150·00
2	Sold Goods for cash	100·00
5	Paid into Bank, cash	90·00
8	Paid E. Wroe by cheque	24·23
	Was allowed discount	1·27
10	Received cheque from A. Wade for . . .	44·14
	Allowed him discount	1·14
14	Sold Goods to T. Neave	200·00
16	Received from T. Neave, cash	95·00
	Allowed him discount	5·00
17	Sold Goods to A. Wade	50·00
20	Bought Goods from W. Bentley	80·50
24	Bought Goods from E. Wroe	50·00
	Bought Typewriter for cash	10·50
26	Received from B. Brown, cash	50·00
	Paid D. Done by cheque	10·53
28	Paid into Bank, cash	60·00
31	Paid Trade Expenses by cash	14·13
	Paid Rent for month by cash	20·00
	Value of Stock (for Ledger only), £416·50.	

QUESTIONS

1. What do you mean by "opening the books"?

2. What is the rule for Journalizing from the Balance Sheet?

3. Why are Assets and Liabilities placed in the position you mention in the previous question?

4. What is Capital?

5. Why was the term "By Sundries" used in posting the amount of C. Pearson's Capital, in the example?

Exercises on Chapter XVII
EXERCISE 47

From the Balance Sheet given below, you are requested to open the books through the Journal; and, afterwards, to enter the transactions as stated in the P.B., S.B., and C.B., post and balance the accounts, prepare a Trial Balance, Profit and Loss Account, and Balance Sheet—

Balance Sheet of Alfred Taylor, on 31st March, 19..

Liabilities	£	Assets	£
C. Brooks	38·50	Cash in hand	55·78
D. Wells	25·75	Cash in Bank	760·50
D. Buck	150·00	Goods in hand	1,200·00
Balance (Capital)	2,411·45	M. Crossley	63·67
		N. Stringer	45·75
		F. Mann	300·00
		P. Hill	200·00
	2,625·70		2,625·70

The following are the transactions for April—

19..		£
Apr 1	Bought Goods for cash	15·00
3	Received from M. Crossley, cheque	61·83
	Allowed him discount	1·84
5	Received cheque from F. Mann, paid into Bank	260·00
7	Sold Goods to N. Stringer	100·00
8	Paid D. Wells, by cheque	24·46
	Was allowed discount	1·29
10	Received from N. Stringer, cheque	44·61
	Allowed him discount	1·14
12	Sold Goods to Brandon & Co.	560·00
14	Received from Brandon & Co. their cheque	546·00
	Allowed them discount	14·00
15	Sold Goods to M. Crossley	250·50
17	Bought Goods from D. Wells	165·75
19	Sent D. Wells cheque	157·46
	Was allowed discount	8·29
24	Paid D. Buck, cheque	100·00
26	Paid C. Brooks, by cheque	38·50
28	Sold Good to Brandon & Co.	200·00
29	Paid Trade Expenses, by cheque	23·25
	Value of Goods unsold (for Ledger only) £340.	

STATEMENT OF ACCOUNT

46 *Bright Street,*
Manchester,

1st April, 19..

Messrs. Byer & Sons,

Warrington.

Dr. to E. SELLERS & Co.

19..				
Jan 2	To Goods		10·33	
9	,, ,,		25·50	
23	,, ,,		5·43	
Feb 16	,, ,,		25·36	
22	,, ,,		40·64	
Mar 15	,, ,,		3·93	
29	,, ,,		14·15	

				125·34
Jan 12	By Returns		5·50	
30	,, Goods		17·50	
Mar 1	,, Cash		25·50	

				48·50

				76·84

STATEMENT OF ACCOUNT

46 Bright Street,
Manchester,

1st Apr., 19..

Messrs. Byer & Sons,
Warrington

Dr. In Account with E. SELLERS & Co. Cr.

19..					19..			
Jan 2	To Goods	.	10·33		Jan 12	By Returns	.	5·50
9	,,	.	25·50		30	Goods	.	17·50
23	,,	.	5·43		Mar 1	Cash	.	25·50
Feb 16	,,	.	25·36		31	Balance	.	76·84
22	,,	.	40·64					
Mar 15	,,	.	3·93					
29	,,	.	14·15					
			125·34					125·34
Apr 1	To Balance	.	76·84					

CHAPTER XVIII

BAD DEBTS

It is, unfortunately, true that almost every firm suffers loss from bad debts. Buyers are sometimes reckless, and purchase beyond their means; or they buy foolishly, paying too high a price for the goods, which they are forced afterwards to sell at a great loss; or sellers are incautious, and allow goods to be delivered without a sufficient guarantee as to the buyer's stability or honesty; or there is a sudden depression in trade, and it is found impossible to convert the goods into cash, with which to pay for them. For these and similar reasons, debtors are sometimes unable to pay their bills; they become *insolvent*, and, after certain formalities in the Court, may be declared *bankrupts.*

It may happen that the bankrupt is unable to pay anything at all towards what he owes to a firm; in which case, of course, the firm loses the whole amount owing by the debtor. He may, however, offer to pay a certain portion of the debt, usually so much in the pound. If this be accepted by his creditors, it is called a *composition.* In this case, the loss to each creditor is not quite so heavy.

In any case, it is necessary to have an account for these losses, and such an account is opened under the heading of **"Bad Debts Account."**

When, therefore, we suffer a loss through a bad debt, we *debit* the Bad Debts Account with the amount of the *loss*, because it *receives* a loss; and *credit* the person who has failed to pay, because he is the *sender*, so to speak, of the loss. If he pays *part* of the debt, we *debit* the cash, if he pays in cash, as is most likely, with the amount *received*; *debit* the Bad Debts Account with the amount of the *loss*; and *credit* the person who has *sent* us the cash and the loss, with the *total amount*.

Suppose, for example, A. Green owes us £100. He fails, or becomes bankrupt, and pays his creditors 50p in the pound.

He sends us £50 in cash, and, of course, we lose £50. The Journal entry would be as follows—

			£ 50·00	£
Bad Debts Account . . . . Dr.			50·00	
To A. Green				50·00

The cash would be entered in the Cash Book as follows—

Dr.   CASH BOOK

	Discount	Cash	Bank
To A. Green . . .		£ 50·00	

In balancing the Ledger, the Bad Debts Account would be *closed* by carrying the balance to the *debit* side of Profit and Loss Account, because it reduces our profit.

It does occasionally happen that a person who has been declared bankrupt afterwards finds himself in a position to pay off the whole of the debts he had left unpaid, and he is scrupulous enough to do so. In such a case, we should *debit* the cash, or Bank, with the amount received and *credit* the Bad Debts Recovered Account, which would also be transferred to the Profit and Loss Account.

The following examples will make the method of dealing with bad debts quite clear—

No. 1   B. Barnes, who owes me £150, has failed. He pays me in cash a composition of 38p in the pound.

2   A. Slowe declared bankrupt. He pays me by cheque 75p in the pound on his debt of £200.

3   Accepted first and final dividend of 50p in the pound on T. Rudman's debt of £75.

4   H. Harris pays me a composition of 75p in the pound on his debt of £40.

5   D. Wrigley, who has failed, owed me £35·53, and there are no assets.

6   Agreed to accept E. Catton's offer of 50p in the pound on his debt of £50, and to write off the balance as a Bad Debt. Received cash £25.

The Journal entries for the preceding examples are shown on page 79.

JOURNAL						Dr.	Cr.
						£	£
No. 1	Bad Debts Account	.	.	*Dr.*		93·00	
	To B. Barnes	.	.	.			93·00
2	Bad Debts Account	.	.	*Dr.*		50·00	
	To A. Slowe	.	.	.			50·00
3	Bad Debts Account	.	.	*Dr.*		37·50	
	To T. Rudman	.	.	.			37·50
4	Bad Debts Account	.	.	*Dr.*		10·00	
	To H. Harris	.	.	.			10·00
5	Bad Debts Account	.	.	*Dr.*		35·53	
	To D. Wrigley	.	.	.			35·53
6	Bad Debts Account	.	.	*Dr.*		25·00	
	To E. Catton	.	.	.			25·00

The Cash Book entries would be as follows—

CASH BOOK

						Discount	Cash	Bank
							£	£
No. 1	To B. Barnes	.	.	.			57·00	
2	A. Slowe	.	.	.				150·00
3	T. Rudman	.	.	.			37·50	
4	H. Harris	.	.	.			30·00	
6	E. Catton	.	.	.			25·00	

QUESTIONS

1. What do you mean by *bankrupt*?

2. Explain some of the ways in which bad debts are brought about.

3. What do you mean by a *composition* of, say, 50p in the £?

4. If you were paid a composition of 75p in the £ on a debt of £100, how much would you receive? What would be your Journal entry for such a case?

5. To what account do you transfer the balance of the Bad Debts Account? Why is this?

6. How much in the £ does 5 per cent discount represent? How much is $2\frac{1}{2}$ per cent? $3\frac{3}{4}$ per cent?

EXERCISES ON CHAPTER XVIII

EXERCISE 48

Enter the following transactions, using Cash Book, Purchases Book, Sales Book and Journal. Post to Ledger. Make out a Trial Balance, Profit and Loss Account, and Balance Sheet.

19..		£
Feb 28	*Assets—*	
	Cash in hand	12·81
	Cash in Bank	1,560·50
	Goods in Stock	2,330·50
	C. Lever	116·50
	D. Saville	68·75
	R. Bell	420·00
	Liabilities—	
	C. Graham	180·00
	M. Abel	150·50
	S. Johnson	863·50
Mar 1	Received from C. Lever, cheque . . .	116·50
3	Sold Goods for cash	73·68
6	Paid M. Abel by cheque	146·74
	Was allowed discount	3·76
8	Sold Goods to C. Lever	220·25
10	Bought Goods from C. Graham . . .	120·00
13	Sold Goods for cash	86·80
15	Paid Trade Expenses by cash . . .	5·75
24	Received cheque form D. Saville . . .	66·78
	Allowed him discount	1·97
28	Sold Goods to D. Saville	180·50
31	Bought Goods for cash	37·25
31	Sold Goods for cash	73·65
31	Paid Trade Expenses by cash . . .	32·61
31	Stock of Goods on hand	1,940·00

EXERCISE 49

Enter in the original books, post, and balance the following. Estimate Goods unsold at £265.

19..		£
Jan 1	S. Brown's Assets were as follows—	
	Cash	10·53
	Bank	360·25
	Goods	750·00
	J. Holmes	260·50
	W. Gay	58·53
	A. Lee	30·75
	And his Liabilities were—	
	To E. Peel	50·53
	H. Hoy	25·26
	J. Wills	106·00

NOTE.—The amount of S. Brown's Capital is, of course, the *difference* between the Liabilities and the Assets.

The following were the transactions for the month—

19..		£
Jan 3	Bought Goods of F. Dawson	100·00
5	Sent F. Dawson cheque for amount of his account, less 5% discount (5% = 5p in the £).	
7	Paid E. Peel's Account by cheque, less 5% discount.	
	Sold Goods for cheque	200·50
12	Accepted composition of 50p in the £ from A. Lee, receiving cash	15·38
14	J. Holmes paid into Bank	160·50
	Sold Goods to C. Conway	150·00
15	Paid H. Hoy, by cheque	25·26
	C. Conway sent cheque	146·25
	Was allowed discount	3·75
21	Sent cheque to J. Wills	106·00
	Sold Goods to K. Simon & Co. . . .	300·00
30	Paid Trade Expenses by cheque . . .	15·50

EXERCISE 50

Enter in the proper books, post, and balance.

ASSETS. May 1. Cash, £52·28; Bank, £500; S. Leefe, £15·75; T. Nash, £260·53; Goods, £700.

LIABILITIES. C. Pearse, £45; L. Jenkins, £110.

			£
19.			
May 2	Sold to G. Sharp, Goods		150·50
4	Bought of Hayes & Co., Goods . . .		85·75
6	Received at Bank, cheque from T. Nash . .		100·53
	G. Sharpe, paid by cheque		60·00
9	S. Leefe, having failed, pays in Cash a composition of 50p in the £		
12	Sent cheque to L. Jenkins		110·00
16	Bought Goods of Hayes & Co. . . .		114·25
17	Paid Hayes & Co. by cheque		190·00
	Was allowed discount		10·00
19	Paid C. Pearse by cheque		45·00
25	Bought Goods of C. Pearse		160·50
	Sold Goods for Cash		100·00
26	Paid into Bank		120·00
30	Paid Trade Expenses by cash		17·46
	Value of Goods unsold		830·50

CHAPTER XIX

DEPRECIATION

In Chapter XVIII we spoke about losses that are almost certain to happen in every business, namely Bad Debts; in this chapter we must deal with another kind of loss which is likely to occur in any business, and that is, that kind of loss that occurs through continued use of an article. For instance, it is well known that a bicycle or a motor-car wears out through continued use; so do tables, chairs, counters, and other office furniture, and it is often necessary that they should be replaced. But if such articles as these wear out, then it is necessary that some note should be made of that fact in the accounts, for we cannot allow an article to stand in the books at the same amount for a number of years when we know that it is of less value. Therefore we open a special account to contain this loss of value and we call it **"Depreciation Account."**

But how is this loss of value through use, passing of time, or other cause, to be ascertained? In some cases, such as loss through the passing of time, the amount of the loss can be easily found, simply by dividing the original amount by the number of years. For instance, take the case of a lease of a shop for seven years for which we paid £980. The lease *decreases* in value regularly through the seven years, and therefore we can decrease the value in our books by an equal amount each year, *i.e.* we should lose one-seventh of £980 each year, namely £140. As we wish to decrease the value in the Lease of Premises Account, which is an asset, we must *credit* it with £140, and being a loss, we *debit* the Depreciation Account with £140.

As there are not usually sufficient entries to justify a special book, we make a Journal Entry, as follows—

19.. Dec 31	Depreciation Account . . . *Dr.* To Lease of Premises Account . .		£ 140·00	£ 140·00

When the items are posted to the Ledger, the accounts will appear as follows—

LEASE OF PREMISES ACCOUNT

Dr. 19.. Dec 31	To Cash	£ 980·00	19.. Dec 31	By Depreciation Balance c/d	Cr. £ 140·00 840·00
		980·00			980·00
19.. Jan 1	To Balance b/d	840·00			

and so on for each year.

DEPRECIATION ACCOUNT

Dr. 19.. Dec 31	To Lease of Premises A/c	£ 140·00	Cr.

In other cases, however, it is not possible to ascertain the amount so easily, for instance, in the case of a motor delivery van which may be kept in good order for five or ten years; and therefore the loss has to be estimated. This is usually done by means of a percentage of the value at the end of each year.

For motor lorries, carts, and vans, the usual rate is from 10 to 15 per cent per annum, for machinery 5 to 10 per cent, for furniture, etc., $2\frac{1}{2}$ to $7\frac{1}{2}$ per cent.

Therefore, in the case of the motor delivery van mentioned above, which may have cost, say, £500, the depreciation, taken at 5 per cent, would be £25 and this amount would be *debited* to the Depreciation Account and *credited* to Motor Vans Account.

At the end of the year after the question of depreciation has been considered, the Depreciation Account, being a loss, is transferred to the Profit and Loss Account.

EXERCISES ON CHAPTER XIX

EXERCISE 51

Enter in the proper books, post, and balance.

June 1

Cash in hand	.	.	£7·75	A. Arnold owes me	. £30·75
Goods	.	.	355·53	T. Kay owes me	. 70·25
Bank	.	.	670·50	I owe E. Leek .	. 10·50
I owe T. Bax	.	.	20·00		

The transactions for June were as follows—

19..		£
Jun 2	Sold Goods for cash	50·00
5	Paid T. Bax by cheque	19·50
	Was allowed discount	0·50
8	T. Kay declared bankrupt. There were no assets	
12	Sold Goods to A. Arnold	69·25
14	Received cheque from A. Arnold to settle his account, less 2½% discount	97·50
16	Sold Goods to W. Farley	80·00
	Bought Goods of T. Bax	49·53
18	Paid E. Leek by cash	9·98
	Was allowed discount	0·52
22	Bought Goods of E. Leek	50·61
25	Sold Goods to A. Arnold	5·27
29	Sold Goods for cash	19·51
	Paid into Bank	50·00
30	Paid Trade Expenses by cash	12·78
	Value of Stock in hand	261·63

EXERCISE 52

Make Journal and Ledger entries on 31st December for the following depreciations. Machinery, value £1,200, rate of depreciation 10 per cent per annum. Delivery vans, value £500, rate of depreciation 12 per cent per annum. Shop fittings, value £350, rate of depreciation 4 per cent per annum.

EXERCISE 53

N. London had on 1st October the following assets and liabilities—

Cash in hand, £11·13; Cash at Bank, £690·50; Stock in hand, £900; Furniture, £150; Machinery, £250; Debtors: C. York, £45; T. Devon, £38. Creditors: D. Ash, £60; A. Bath, £80. Enter the above, and the following transactions in the proper books, make a Trial Balance, Profit and Loss Account, and Balance Sheet.

			£
19..			
Oct	1	Sold Goods to C. York	22·43
	3	Bought Goods from D. Ash	30·50
	5	Received cheque from C. York, £43; Discount, £2 .	45·00
	6	Sold Goods to T. Devon	35·48
	9	Sent cheque to D. Ash, £40; received Discount, £1·50	41·50
	10	T. Devon returned Goods	1·48
	12	Sold Goods to G. Lancaster	50·00
	13	Sent cheque to A. Bath	45·52
	16	T. Devon sent cheque, £29·50; Discount, £1·25	30·75
	17	Bought Goods from M. Selby	57·50
	19	Sent cheque to A. Bath, £33; Discount, £1·48 .	34·48
		Drew cheque for Office Cash	10·00
		Paid various Expenses in cash	14·28
		Depreciation of Furniture	7·50
		Depreciation of Machinery	20·00
		Stock in hand	920·00

CHAPTER XX

THE TRADING AND PROFIT AND LOSS ACCOUNTS

In Chapter IX we saw how the accounts for goods were balanced, and we found that before we could do this, we had to find the value of the goods unsold. It has also happened in some exercises that in addition to credit purchases and sales, there have been cash purchases and cash sales, and in some cases there have been returns either inward or outward. If these were combined into one account it would be difficult to tell what the total or net purchases and sales were without making a separate addition or subtraction on another slip of paper. Most traders like to be able to compare their total and net purchases and total and net sales for any month with previous months, so that they can see, among other things, whether their turnover is increasing or decreasing, and whether their purchases are keeping steady or increasing correspondingly. In order to have this information available, it is usual to open separate accounts for the purchases and sales, and returns inwards and returns outwards, and as that leaves only the goods in hand at the beginning and end of the period, it is usual to enter these in the "Stock Account." Assuming the following transactions: stock, 1st Jan., £160; cash purchases, 10th Jan., £25, 21st Jan., £17; month's credit purchases, £275; cash sales, 8th Jan., £40, 19th Jan., £31; month's credit sales, £370; returns inwards £30, returns outwards £22. The accounts, as before stocktaking, would then appear as follows—

Dr.   PURCHASES ACCOUNT   *Cr.*

19..		£
Jan 10	To Cash . . .	25·00
21	,, . . .	17·00
31	Purchases as per Purchases Book .	275·00

87

Dr.   SALES ACCOUNT   *Cr.*

		£
19..		
Jan 8	By Cash . . .	40·00
19	„ . . .	31·00
31	Sales as per Sales	
	Book . . .	370·00

Dr.   RETURNS INWARDS ACCOUNT   *Cr.*

19..		£	
Jan 31	To Returns . .	30·00	

Dr.   RETURNS OUTWARDS ACCOUNT   *Cr.*

			£
	19..		
	Jan 31	By Returns . .	22·00

Dr.   STOCK ACCOUNT   *Cr.*

19..		£	
Jan 1	To Goods in hand .	160·00	

These entries would, of course, be posted from the subsidiary books, viz., C.B., P.B., S.B., R.I.B., R.O.B., and Journal. But now, how are we to find the profit? It is found in this way: at the end of the month, or whatever period the trader pleases, a new account, called the "Trading Account" is opened, and to it are transferred all the accounts relating to "Goods," these accounts being balanced or "closed." To make the transfer, we must first of all have a Journal entry.

In the case of the Stock Account, for example, the goods in hand on 1st Jan. are on the *debit* side, and this amount is transferred to the *debit* side of the Trading Account. But we cannot have a debit for the same item in two accounts, and therefore the debit in the Stock Account must be cancelled by a *credit* entry showing that the amount has been transferred to the Trading Account. Our Journal entry will be as follows.

JOURNAL

19..								£	£
Jan 31	Trading Account	*Dr.*	160·00	
	To Stock Account			160·00

And this, when posted, will appear as follows—

Dr.		STOCK ACCOUNT		*Cr.*
19.. Jan 1	To Goods in hand .	£ 160·00	19.. Jan 31 By Trading Account .	£ 160·00

Dr.		TRADING ACCOUNT	*Cr.*
19.. Jan 31	To Stock Account .	£ 160·00	

The Purchases Account and the Returns Inwards Account will need exactly similar Journal entries to close them. The Sales Account and the Returns Outwards Account having the items on the credit side will need a *debit* entry in that account and a *credit* entry in the Trading Account.

We must now deal with the figure obtained at stocktaking as the value of the goods in hand at the end of the period. We have seen (page 34) that in order to find the profit or loss the stock in hand had to be entered in the Trading Account; we must credit it with the value of the stock in hand, which we will suppose to be £180. We must not, however, have a credit without a debit, or vice versa, and therefore, since the £180 represents goods which belong to us, we debit the Stock Account, and so obtain our double entry.

The full Journal entries are as follows—

19..									£	£
Jan 31	Trading Account .	.	.	.	.	.	*Dr.*		160·00	
	To Stock Account	.	.	.	.	.	.			160·00
	Trading Account .	.	.	.	.	.	*Dr.*		317·00	
	To Purchases Account	.	.	.	.	.				317·00
	Trading Account .	.	.	.	.	.	*Dr.*		30·00	
	To Returns Inwards Account	.	.	.	.				30·00
	Sales Account	.	.	.	.	.	*Dr.*		441·00	
	To Trading Account .	.	.	.	.	.				441·00
	Returns Outwards Account	.	.	.	.	*Dr.*		22·00	
	To Trading Account .	.	.	.	.	.				22·00
	Stock Account	.	.	.	.	.	*Dr.*		180·00	
	To Trading Account .	.	.	.	.	.				180·00

When the items are posted the accounts will appear as follows.

Dr.   STOCK ACCOUNT   *Cr.*

19..		£	19..		£
Jan 1	To Goods in hand .	160·00	Jan 31	By Trading A/c . .	160·00
Jan 31	To Goods in hand .	180·00			

Dr.   PURCHASES ACCOUNT   *Cr.*

19..		£	19..		£
Jan 10	To Cash . . .	25·00	Jan 31	By Trading A/c . .	317·00
21	,,	17·00			
31	Purchases as per Purchases Book .	275·00			
		317·00			317·00

Dr.   RETURNS INWARDS ACCOUNT   *Cr.*

19..		£	19..		£
Jan 31	To Returns . .	30·00	Jan 31	By Trading A/c .	30·00

Dr.   RETURNS OUTWARDS ACCOUNT   *Cr.*

19..		£	19..		£
Jan 31	To Trading A/c . .	22·00	Jan 31	By Returns . .	22·00

Dr.   SALES ACCOUNT   *Cr.*

19..		£	19..		£
Jan 31	To Trading A/c . .	441·00	Jan 8	By Cash . .	40·00
			19	,, . .	31·00
			31	Sales as per Sales Book . .	370·00
		441·00			441·00

Dr.   TRADING ACCOUNT   *Cr.*

19..		£	19..		£
Jan 31	To Stock . .	160·00	Jan 31	By Sales . .	441·00
	Purchases . .	317·00		Returns Outwards .	22·00
	Returns Inwards .	30·00		Stock . .	180·00
	Profit & Loss .	136·00			
		643·00			643·00

The figure of £136 is obtained by subtracting the total of the debit side from the total of the credit side, and, of course, the difference represents the Gross Profit, which is transferred to the Profit and Loss Account. The Profit and Loss Account, too, deals only with *totals* of the items of profits and losses. Separate accounts should be opened for Rent Account, Wages Account, Interest Received Account, and for other items of profit or loss, as the case may be. Each of these accounts would be closed by transferring the total amount at the end of the month or other period to the Profit and Loss Account. Thus, taking the Wages Account as an example, and supposing the wages paid to be £10 per week, the account before being closed would appear as follows—

Dr.		WAGES ACCOUNT				Cr.
			£	19..		£
19..						
Jan 8	To Cash .	.	. 10·00			
15	,, .	.	. 10·00			
22	,, .	.	. 10·00			
29	,, .	.	. 10·00			

In order to close the account and transfer the total amount we shall need a Journal entry. Since in the Wages Account the items have been debited, a *credit* entry will be needed to make both sides equal, and being a loss, the Profit and Loss Account must be *debited*. The Journal entry will therefore be as follows—

JOURNAL

19..								£	£
Jan 31	Profit & Loss Account	.	.	.	.	. Dr.		40·00	
	To Wages Account	.	.	.	.	.			40·00

After this item has been posted the accounts will appear as follows—

Dr.		WAGES ACCOUNT			Cr.
19..		£			£
Jan 8	To Cash . . . 10·00		Jan 31	By Profit & Loss	
15	,, . . . 10·00			Account . .	40·00
22	,, . . . 10·00				
29	,, . . . 10·00				
		40·00			40·00

4·

Dr.		PROFIT AND LOSS ACCOUNT			Cr.

		£			£
19.. Jan 31	To Wages A/c . Capital A/c .	40·00 96·00	Jan 31	By Trading A/c . .	136·00
		136·00			136·00

The amount of £96 is the difference between the two sides and represents the net profit to the owner of the business. When separate accounts are opened for Stock, Purchases, and Sales, and for the items of expense, the Trading and the Profit and Loss Accounts are not opened until after the Trial Balance has been found to agree, that is, that the Dr and Cr. sides are equal.

TRIAL BALANCE

							Dr. £	Cr. £
Debtors: T. Mann	.	.	.	.			170·00	
H. Venn	.	.	.	.			216·00	
Opening Stock	.	.	.	,	.	T.	487·00	
Creditors: M. Dunn	.	.	.	.				187·00
P. Hann	.	.	.	.				97·00
Furniture	.	.	.	.	.		100·00	
Purchases	.	.	.	-	.	T.	840·00	
Salaries	.	.	.	,	.		74·00	
Carriage on Purchases	.	.	.	,	T.		30·00	
Returns Inwards	.	.	.	.	T.		10·00	
Bad Debts	.	.	.	.	.		22·00	
Sales	.	,	.	,	,	T.		1,210·00
Rent and Rates	.	.	.	-	.		63·00	
Returns Outwards	.	.	.	.	T.			15·00
Bank Balance	.	.	.	.	.		61·00	
Discount	.	.	.	,	.		13·00	
Capital	.	.	.	.	.			632·00
Office Expenses	.	,	.	.	,		55·00	
							2,141·00	2,141·00

Closing Stock, £477
Depreciate Furniture, 5% p.a.

TRADING AND PROFIT AND LOSS ACCOUNT FOR THE YEAR
ENDING . . .

Dr.					Cr.
	£	£		£	£
To Stock . . .		487·00	By Sales .	1,210·00	
Purchases	840·00		Less Re-		
Less Re-			turns	10·00	1,200·00
turns	15·00	825·00			
			Stock . .		477·00
Carriage . . .		30·00			
Gross Profit c/d. .		335·00			
		1,677·00			1,677·00

		£		£
To Rent and Rates .		63·00	By Gross Profit b/d. .	335·00
Salaries . .		74·00		
Office Expenses .		55·00		
Bad Debts . .		22·00		
Discount . . .		13·00		
Depreciation . .		5·00		
Net Profit . .		103·00		
		335·00		335·00

It will be seen that since these "closing" entries, as they are
called, are not made until after the Trial Balance has been
agreed, and as the Trial Balance contains the balances of the
accounts, therefore these entries can be made direct from the
information contained in the Trial Balance. Consequently
the Trading, the Profit and Loss Account, and the Balance
Sheet can be compiled from the Trial Balance without
referring to the actual accounts.

We have seen earlier in this Chapter that the debit balances
of the Stock Account and the Purchases Account are placed
on the debit side of the Trading Account; and the credit
balance of the Sales Account is placed on the credit side of the
Trading Account. Therefore, it is a simple matter for us to
extract the figures and place them in the Trading Account on
the same side as they are in the Trial Balance. Similarly with
the Profit and Loss Account. In the case of the Balance Sheet,
however, the rule is slightly different. Debit balances of
accounts are placed on the Assets side of the Balance Sheet,

that is, the right-hand side, which in an account is the credit; while credit balances of accounts are placed on the Liabilities side of the Balance Sheet, the left-hand side, which in an account is the debit. But the Balance Sheet is *not* an account and the items in the Trial Balance relating to the Balance Sheet must be placed on the opposite side to that on which they are in the Trial Balance. Let us take an example.

Assume we have just completed the Trial Balance on page 92.

We must now pick out the items which are placed in the Trading Account; Stock, Purchases, Sales, and the Returns Accounts are obvious, but the item "Carriage in Purchases" may be doubtful. The title of the account indicates that a charge has been made for the conveyance of goods from the sellers to ourselves, and the cost of the goods has consequently been increased. Therefore the item is placed in the Trading Account, which appears on page 93.

Note that the Returns Inwards and Outwards Accounts are deducted from the Purchases and Sales items in the Trading Account, instead of being placed on the debit and credit sides. The effect is the same; they are arranged in this manner to show the net purchases and net sales. In actual business the Profit and Loss Account is joined to the Trading Account in the manner shown instead of having a separate heading.

It will be seen that the remaining items in the Trial Balance are Debtors and Creditors, Bank Balance, and Capital. The preparation of the Final Accounts, as the Trading and Profit and Loss Accounts are sometimes called, is considerably helped if a letter T or P, or a tick, is marked in the Trial Balance when the item has been placed in the Trading or Profit and Loss Account, as has been done in this example for the Trading Account. The remaining items will be those to be inserted in the Balance Sheet, which will appear as shown on page 95.

In actual business the names of the Debtors and Creditors are not inserted in the Balance Sheet, only the totals of separate lists being inserted. The student should also notice that items in the Trial Balance are only inserted once in the Final

BALANCE SHEET AS AT ...

Liabilities		£	Assets		£
Creditors: M. Dunn	.	187·00	Bank Balance . .		61·00
P. Hann	.	97·00	Debtors: T. Mann .		170·00
Capital Account—			H. Venn .		216·00
Balance .	632·00		Stock . . .		477·00
Add Net Profit	103·00		Furniture .	100·00	
		735·00	*Less* Depreci-		
			ation .	5·00	
					95·00
		1,019·00			1,019·00

Accounts and Balance Sheet, but an item outside the Trial Balance, such as Closing Stock in this example, must be inserted twice, once in the Trading or Profit and Loss Account and once in the Balance Sheet, in order to fulfil the Double Entry.

EXERCISES ON CHAPTER XX
EXERCISE 54

From the following particulars prepare Purchases, Sales, Stock, Rent, Wages, Discount, Trading, and Profit and Loss Accounts for March, closing the accounts by means of Journal entries.

Cash sales, £54; credit sales, £147; credit purchases, £120; cash purchases, £36; stock on 1st March, £175, and on 31st March, £200; the rent for the month was £10; the wages were £10 per week; the discount allowed to me was £7·50, while I allowed my debtors £5.

EXERCISE 55

From the following particulars prepare Trading and Profit and Loss Accounts for the month of June.

Total Purchases, £132·15; total sales, £201·20; Trade Expenses Account, £6·51; Wages Account, £26·50; Discount Account, £0·95 (allowed to me). The stock on hand at 30th June was £20.

CHAPTER XXI

REVISION

BEFORE entering upon a further part of our study it will be well for us to review our past work, and see what we know of the subject thus far. We shall then be better prepared to go farther.

We have learned, then, that the great principle of Double Entry Book-keeping is that every debit entry must have a corresponding credit entry, so that the sum of the *debits* should equal the sum of the *credits*, and that where this is not the case there must be an error in our work somewhere. The system, therefore, reduces the liability to err, and when a mistake is committed, it is almost certain to be discovered in time to be remedied.

In applying the principle just referred to, we followed the rule that the *receiving* account is made *debtor* to the *sending* or *delivering* account for whatever was sent or delivered; that is, Cash, Goods, etc. This rule we shall continue to follow in the transactions to be dealt with in the following chapters.

We have seen that in actual business there are certain subsidiary books used to facilitate entries in the Ledger; namely, *Cash Book, Purchases Book, Sales Book, Returns Inwards,* and *Returns Outwards Books,* and *Journal.* There are other subsidiary books in addition to these, according to the particular requirements of each business, but the method of using them is much the same, and the student will find it easy to adapt his knowledge to the circumstances of the case, as may be necessary. As a matter of fact, the Cash Book is strictly a part of the Ledger, and it is only because there are so many entries for cash that a special book is provided for them.

Our Balance Sheet, it will be remembered, showed us, in a very brief form, the state of our affairs after recording a set of transactions. The difference between the two sides of the Balance Sheet, that is to say, the *balance*, represented what we were worth: and as this constituted our *capital*, it should, of course, always agree with the balance of our Capital Account. Where this was found to be the case, we rightly regarded it as a further proof of the accuracy of our work.

And now we may go a little farther in our study, and see something of other transactions that occur in business and the method of dealing with them. We shall, however, have nothing to unlearn. On the contrary, the principles we have mastered so far will be applied in treating the new features as they arise.

QUESTIONS

1. What is Double Entry?
2. How does it ensure accuracy in our work?
3. What rule is to be followed in applying the Double Entry principle?
4. Why is a special book provided for cash?
5. What does the balance of the Balance Sheet represent?
6. With what account should it agree?

EXERCISE 56

From the following prepare Trading and Profit and Loss Accounts. Stock on hand, £1,950; Depreciation of Furniture, 10 per cent per annum.

TRIAL BALANCE, 31ST DECEMBER

	£	£
Stock, 1st January	2,177·00	
Rent and Rates	450·00	
Furniture	300·00	
Sales		3,100·00
General Expenses	87·00	
Debtors	795·00	
Capital		2,800·00
Purchases	1,575·00	
Cash in hand	391·00	
Returns Inwards	105·00	
Bad Debts	48·00	
Returns Outwards		125·00
Carriage on Purchases	67·00	
Salaries	400·00	
Creditors		370·00
	6,395·00	6,395·00

EXERCISE 57

F. P. McIntosh began business on 1st March with the following Assets and Liabilities.

Cash in hand, £50·70; Cash at Bank, £957·40; Debtors: T. Wilson, £90·23; W. Tapper, £36·38; M. Hay, £160. Creditors: A. Hunter, £47·23; N. Farrer, £89·50 and Stock, £500.

Find his Capital and then enter the following transactions in the Books of Original Entry, and make out Trial Balance, Trading and Profit and Loss Accounts, and Balance Sheet.

19..		£
Mar 1	Sold Goods to T. Wilson	45·38
2	Received cheque from M. Hay	90·00
	Bought Goods from T. Cadman	53·32
3	Paid N. Farrer, cheque	49·50
5	Received letter from W. Tapper saying he is insolvent and enclosing cheque for	18·19
	Wrote off remainder as Bad Debt	
6	Paid Wages in cash	14·50
	Returned Goods to T. Cadman	4·53
8	Sent A. Hunter, cheque	40·00
9	Sold Goods for cash	21·50
10	Bought Goods from A. Hunter	38·75
11	Sold Goods to J. Cullum	70·00
	Paid Trade Expenses in cash	9·50
12	Received cheque from T. Wilson	40·00
	Allowed him discount	2·23
13	Paid Wages in Cash	14·50
	Stock in hand	400·00

CHAPTER XXII

BILLS OF EXCHANGE

A Bill of Exchange is an unconditional order in writing, addressed by one person to another, for the payment of a specified sum of money, at a fixed date, to some person named, or to the bearer.

All Bills of Exchange must bear a stamp, adhesive or impressed.

Bills are either *Inland* or *Foreign*. An **Inland Bill** is one drawn by a person resident within the British Isles upon another person also resident within the same place: as a bill drawn by a person in Manchester upon a person in London.

A **Foreign Bill** is one drawn by a person resident in one country upon another person resident in some other country: as a bill drawn by a firm in Liverpool upon a firm in Calcutta.

The following is a specimen of an Inland Bill—

£66·53	*Due 11th May.*	*London, 8th February*, 19..
	Three months after date pay to me or my order the sum of Sixty-six	
STAMP	*Pounds* 53 *sterling for value received.*	
	To Mr. Thomas Benson,	*James Robinson.*
	Manchester.	

This bill is drawn by James Robinson upon Thomas Benson. The person who draws or makes out the bill is called the *drawer*; the person upon whom it is drawn is called the *drawee*. The *drawee* is the person who will have to *pay*; the *drawer* is the person who will *receive* the amount. In its present form the document is called a *draft*; and in this state it is sent by James Robinson to Thomas Benson to be signed, or, as it is called, *accepted*. When T. Benson receives the draft, if he is willing to pay as directed on the form, he writes on the paper, and generally, across the face of it, the word "accepted," together with his name, and, very likely, the name of his bank where the amount will be paid. The draft has now become an *acceptance*, and, because he has *accepted* it, T. Benson is called the *acceptor*. In its altered form it is returned to the drawer, *James Robinson*.

The following is a specimen of an **Acceptance**—

£66·53   *Due 11th May.*   *London, 8th February, 19..*

        Three months after date pay to me or my order the sum of Sixty-six

        Pounds 53 sterling for value received.

STAMP

          To Mr. Thomas Benson,   *James Robinson.*

             Manchester.

Since J. Robinson is to *receive* the amount of the bill, it is to *him* a **Bill Receivable**; but, because Thomas Benson will have to *pay* it, it is to *him* a **Bill Payable**. There is, therefore, a twofold aspect to every bill; it is at once both a Bill Receivable and a Bill Payable, according as it is looked at from the point of view of the *drawer* or the *drawee*.

It will be noticed that the bill is due on the 11th of May, three months and *three* days from the 8th of February.

The three extra days allowed for the payment of the bill are called *days of grace*.

Suppose, however, that J. Robinson desires to obtain money for the bill before the date on which it falls due. He can do so by taking it to a banker, who will cash it for him, giving him the amount stated in the bill *less* his charge for cashing it. Such a proceeding is called *discounting* the bill, and the amount charged by the banker is called *discount*. Or, if he wishes, J. Robinson may pay the bill away to someone else to whom he owes money. In this case, he *endorses* it, that is, he writes his name across the back of the bill, which then becomes a negotiable document, and may be passed from one person to another, each one endorsing it in turn, until, eventually, it is presented, on the 11th of May, for payment at the bank mentioned by the original acceptor, T. Benson.

Bills may be drawn at Sight or at a stated time after sight. The following is a specimen—

£70·50   *Leeds, 8th May, 19. .*

STAMP	*Fourteen days after sight pay to me or my order the sum of Seventy Pounds 50 sterling for value received.*
	    To Mr. William Wood, *George Gragson.*
	      75 Arthur Street, London, E.C.4.

When Mr. Wood receives this document for *sighting*, or *accepting*, he signs his name across it, as in the previous case, and adds the date on which he does so. The bill will fall due three days after the expiration of the time stated, and, like the previous bill, it may be negotiated, paid away, or discounted.

Foreign Bills are usually drawn in sets of three, and sent abroad by different mails, so that in case the first gets lost by any means, the second or third may be safely delivered. When *one* of the three reaches the person upon whom it is drawn, the others are, of course, of no value.

The following is a specimen of a Foreign Bill—

No. 564.
£450·78

Due. . . . . .
Bombay, 4th April, 19. .

STAMP	*At four months after sight of this our First of Exchange (second and third of same tenor and date being unpaid) pay to the order of Charles Cookson the sum of Four Hundred and Fifty Pounds 78 sterling, value received.*

To Messrs. Dunn, Evans & Co.,   *Blake, White & Co.*
      London.

This bill is endorsed by Mr. Cookson, and presented by him, or his agents, to Messrs. Dunn, Evans & Co., to be *sighted*, and in due time it is presented for payment.

There is another form of bill called a **Promissory Note.**

It is, as its name implies, a *promise* to pay a certain sum of money, on a specified date, to the person whose name appears on the document, or to the order of such person. It will be noticed that a Promissory Note is *drawn* and is *payable* by the *same person*. In this it differs from a Bill of Exchange, which is *drawn* by one person, and *payable* by another. A Promissory Note, however, may be used exactly like an Acceptance, and in Book-keeping it is treated as such.

The following is a specimen of a Promissory Note—

£150   *Birmingham, 8th June,* 19..

| STAMP | *Two months after date, I promise to pay to Mr. Edward Henshaw, or order, the sum of One Hundred and Fifty Pounds sterling for value received.* |

Samuel Kennedy.

In the Promissory Note just given, Samuel Kennedy is both the *drawer* and the *payer*; the amount, however, will be *received* by Edward Henshaw, and, therefore, to Edward Henshaw it is a Bill *Receivable*, while to Samuel Kennedy it is a Bill *Payable*.

A further example of a Promissory Note is given below. It will be noted that the promise is to pay *on demand*. No days of grace are allowed on notes drawn on demand.

£300   *London, 8th June,* 19..

| STAMP | *On demand I promise to pay James Eckersley, or order, the sum of Three Hundred Pounds sterling value received.* |

Charles Dixon.

Bills of Exchange are very useful in commerce. They *settle the time* when a debt is to be paid; they are *negotiable documents*, and may be turned into ready money, by *discounting*, as soon as they are received, if this is desired; they are *convenient representatives of money*, and may be sent through the post with little or no risk, as in case of loss the payment of a bill may be stopped at the bank, and a new bill sent.

QUESTIONS

1. What is a Bill of Exchange?
2. How many kinds of bills are there?
3. What is an Inland Bill? A Foreign Bill?
4. Write out a form of Inland Bill, drawn by yourself upon Bernard Smith, of London, for the sum of £50, and payable in three months.

EXERCISES ON CHAPTER XXII
EXERCISE 58

On January, 19.., Alfred Smith, of Manchester, draws upon Edward Roberts, London, at two months' date for £160·78. Make out the bill as accepted by E. Roberts, and say when it will be due.

EXERCISE 59

On 8th March, 19.., Messrs. Crews, Smith & Co., of London, drew upon Messrs. Slatin & Sons, of Calcutta, requesting them to pay to the order of Messrs. Brown, Umber & Co., at four months after sight, the sum of £1,200. Draw the bill, as the *first* of the set of three, and say *why* Foreign Bills are usually drawn in sets of three.

EXERCISE 60

On 14th November, 19.., James Hughes, of Huddersfield, gave a Promissory Note, at one month's date, to Arthur Dawson, for the sum of £25·53. Draw out the Promissory Note, and say when it would be mature.

CHAPTER XXIII

THE BILLS BOOKS

WHEN we *accept* a bill we become liable for its payment, and it is to *us* a Bill *Payable*. The fact of having *accepted* a bill would be recorded in a **Bills Payable Book,** ruled as in the specimen given, with columns for the various particulars required. When we receive an *acceptance* from someone else, or when we *draw* (a bill) upon someone else, such an acceptance or bill would be to *us* a Bill *Receivable*, and this would be recorded in the **Bills Receivable Book,** made out as in the specimen. The headings of the columns will explain their use.

Let us take the following Bill transactions and enter them in their proper places in the Bill Books—

EXERCISE 61

19··			£
Jan 1	Received from W. Mason his Acceptance at two months		150·00
8	Accepted G. Jones's Draft payable in a month .	.	70·53
15	Gave J. Wild my Acceptance at four months .	.	200·00
19	Bought of Sands & Co., for three months' Bill, Goods		75·00
25	Received from C. Cliffe his Acceptance at three months		50·75
28	Sold to W. Berry, Goods, and received his Bill at one month in payment	.	80·53
30	Accepted A. Adam's Draft at two months .	.	40·63

NOTES ON EXERCISE 61

On 1st January, we received from W. Mason *his* Acceptance, that is, his undertaking to *pay*. This is to *us* a Bill Receivable. On the 8th, *we* accept G. Jones's Draft, and so become liable for its *payment*; it is, therefore, to us a Bill Payable. On the 15th, we give J. Wild *our* Acceptance or undertaking to pay, and this, too, is a Bill Payable. On the 19th, we buy goods and pay for them with a Bill, on which, at the proper time, we

BILLS RECEIVABLE

L.F. No.	Date when received	Drawer	Acceptor	Of whom received	Where payable	Date when accepted	Term	When due	Amount £	When due (Jan–Dec)	Remarks
1	19.. Jan 1	Self	W. Mason	W. Mason	London	Jan 1	2 mos.	Mar 4	150·00	Mar 4	
2	25	,,	C. Cliffe	C. Cliffe	Leeds	,, 25	3 ,,	Apr 28	50·75	Apr 28	
3	28	,,	W. Berry	W. Berry	Hull	,, 28	1 mo.	Mar 3	80·53	Mar 3	

BILLS PAYABLE

L.F. No.	Date when accepted	To whom given	Where payable	Term	When due	Amount £	When due (Jan–Dec)	Remarks
1	19.. Jan 8	G. Jones	Liverpool	1 mo.	Feb 11	70·53	Feb 11	
2	15	J. Wild	,,	4 mos.	May18	200·00	May 18	
3	19	Sands & Co.	,,	3 ,,	Apr 22	75·00	Apr 22	
4	30	A. Adams	,,	2 ,,	2	40·63	2	

shall have to pay the amount stated. The transaction on the 25th is similar to that on the 1st. On the 28th we *sell* to W. Berry goods valued at £80·53, and receive his bill in payment. W. Berry will have to pay this, so that it is, to *us*, a Bill Receivable. The item on the 30th is the same as that on the 8th. When these are entered up, our Bills Books should appear as shown on page 105.

QUESTIONS

1. When I *accept* a draft, is it to *me* a B.P. (Bill Payable) or a B.R. (Bill Receivable)?

2. When G. Gray sends me *his* Acceptance, is it to *him* a B.P. or B.R.?

3. When I *draw* upon E. Kay, and he *accepts*, is the bill, as regards *me*, a B.P. or B.R.?

4. What are "days of grace"?

5. When would a three months' sight bill be due which was accepted on 7th Feb.? (Always calculate as *calendar* months.)

EXERCISES ON CHAPTER XXIII

EXERCISE 62

From the following particulars compile Bills Books—

19..		£
Feb 1	Drew on J. Kay at one month (*We* draw, he *accepts*) .	100·00
6	W. Moss drew on us at three months (*He* draws, *we* accept)	50·50
12	Received from K. Moore his Acceptance at four months	85·75
19	Gave E. Lee our Acceptance at one month . .	45·28
20	Accepted G. Roe's Draft at three months . . .	150·00
21	Received from W. Ball, J. Martin's Acceptance at one month	35·50
	(This is to us a Bill Receivable. The fact that J. Martin will eventually have to pay it does not affect our entry, except that in the column for "Acceptor" we write "J. Martin"; and in the column for "Drawer," "W. Ball.")	
28	Gave S. Sly our Acceptance at two months . .	60·53

EXERCISE 63

From the following statement compile Bills Books—

19..		£
Mar 1	Received of William Stainer his Acceptance at two months	100·00
8	Accepted A. Swift's Draft at three months . .	250·00
12	Received of B. Wrigley his Promissory Note at one month	75·00
16	Gave S. Cook my Acceptance at four months . .	150·50
23	Received of F. Hurst, E. King's Acceptance at three months	86·80
30	Accepted H. Lever's Draft at one month . . .	120·00
Apr 1	Drew on I. Jay at a month, and he accepted next day	60·30
8	Accepted W. Morgan's Draft at two months . .	120·60
14	Received Bill at three months from K. Bealey . .	180·25
18	J. Green drew on me at two months' date, and I accepted his Draft	270·00
23	Gave my Bill at one month to A. Deal . . .	55·75
28	O. Mars accepted my Draft at one month . .	90·50

CHAPTER XXIV

POSTING THE BILLS BOOKS

THE Bills Books are posted to the Ledger in exactly the same way as the Purchases Book and the Sales Book. When a person gives us a bill, we enter the particulars of it in the Bills Receivable Book, and *credit* the account of the person who gave us the bill; thus, "By B.R., so much." At the end of the month the total amount of the bills received is transferred to the Dr. side of the "Bills Receivable Account" in the Ledger, where it is entered thus: "To Bills Received, so much." In the same way, when *we* give a bill to a person, it is entered in the Bills Payable Book, and the account of the person to whom we gave the bill is *debited* with the amount of it. At the end of the month the total amount of Bills Payable is transferred to the Cr. side of "Bills Payable Account" in the Ledger, where it is entered thus: "By Bills Granted, so much." Thus we have a *debit* and a *credit* for the bill transactions in the Ledger.

EXERCISE 64

From the following particulars compile Bills Books, and post them into Ledger, as directed above.

19··		£
Mar 1	Received from F. Hall his Acceptance at one month .	65·75
5	Gave G. Hawker my Acceptance at two months .	110·53
8	Drew on I. Irving at three months' date for . .	50·00
10	J. James accepted my Draft at three months for .	90·00
14	Received from F. Hall his Acceptance at two months .	30·00
19	Gave G. Hawker my Acceptance at one month .	45·78
21	J. James gives me his Acceptance at one month for .	35·50
28	Accepted W. Young's Draft at two months' date .	80·00

When Exercise 64 has been completed, the result will be as shown below; the names of the places would be on the bills. It will be seen, too, that the date on which a bill is *received* may be different from that on which it was *accepted*. The difference would be caused by the time spent in transmitting the bill through the post.

LEDGER

Dr.	F. HALL, BOLTON	Cr.
	19..	£
	Mar 1 By Bill Rec. . .	65·75
	14 ,, ,, . .	30·00

Dr.	G. HAWKER, LONDON	Cr.
19..	£	
Mar 5 To Bill Pay . .	110·53	
19 ,, ,, . .	45·78	

Dr.	I. IRVING, HALIFAX	Cr.
	19..	£
	Mar 8 By Bill Rec. . .	50·00

Dr.	J. JAMES, LEEDS	Cr.
	19..	£
	Mar 10 By Bill Rec. . .	90·00
	21 ,, ,, . .	35·50

Dr.	W. YOUNG, LONDON	Cr.
19..	£	
Mar 28 To Bill Pay . .	80·00	

Dr.	BILLS RECEIVABLE ACCOUNT	Cr.
19..	£	
Mar 31 To Bills Rec. . .	271·25	

Dr.	BILLS PAYABLE ACCOUNT	Cr.
	19..	£
	Mar 31 By Bills Granted . .	236·31

BILLS RECEIVABLE BOOK

L.F. No.	Date when received	Drawer	Acceptor	Of whom received	Where payable	Date when accepted	Term	When due	Amount £	Jan	Feb	Mar	Apr	May	Jun	Jul	Aug	Sep	Oct	Nov	Dec	Remarks
1	19.. Mar 1	Self	F. Hall	F. Hall	Bolton	19.. Mar 1	1 mo.	Apr 4	65·75				4									
2	10	"	I. Irving	I. Irving	Halifax	8	3 mos.	Jun 11	50·00						11							
3	10	"	J. James	J. James	Leeds	10	3 "	13	90·00						13							
4	14	"	F. Hall	F. Hall	Bolton	14	2 "	May17	30·00					17								
5	21	"	J. James	J. James	Leeds	21	1 mo.	Apr 24	35·50				24									
							To Bills Received		271·25													

BILLS PAYABLE BOOK

L.F. No.	Date when accepted	To whom given	Where payable	Term	When due	Amount £	Jan	Feb	Mar	Apr	May	Jun	Jul	Aug	Sep	Oct	Nov	Dec	Remarks
1	19.. Mar 6	G. Hawker	London	2 mos.	May 8	110·53					8								
2	19	"	"	1 mo.	Apr 22	45·78				22									
3	28	W. Young	"	2 mos.	May31	80·00					31								
				By Bills Granted		236·61													

QUESTIONS

1. How do you post the Bills Books?

2. On which side of the Bills Receivable Account do you enter the total amount of bills received?

3. What is a Promissory Note? Would you treat it as a bill?

4. How does a Promissory Note differ from a Bill of Exchange?

5. Explain why a bill may be received on a different date from that on which it has been *accepted*.

6. What do you mean by "accepting" a bill?

7. State some of the advantages of bills in trade.

8. Which account would be credited if *you* accept a bill?

EXERCISES ON CHAPTER XXIV
EXERCISE 65

Compile Bills Books, and post same into Ledger.

19..			£
Apr 1	Drew on G. Lever at two months for . . .		100·00
5	Accepted F. Lakin's Draft at three months for . .		89·50
8	W. Moss accepted my Draft at one month for .		66·78
10	A. Bell gave me his Promissory Note, due in two months for		40·53
15	Gave B. Eccles my Acceptance at four months for .		200·00
22	Received from E. Delves his Acceptance at one month		70·00
29	S. Taylor accepted my Draft at three months for .		50·50

EXERCISE 66

From the following, compile Bills Books, and post into Ledger—

19..		£
May 1	Received from A. Bigley his Acceptance at two months	160·50
6	Accepted R. Moore's Draft at one month . . .	100·00
12	D. Ingham drew on me at three months, and I accepted his Draft	260·53
13	J. Lander accepted my Draft at two months . .	89·75
18	Gave A. Samson my Bill at three months . . .	60·13
24	Accepted E. Mill's Draft at one month . . .	40·29
28	Gave my Bill at two months to C. Drury . . .	56·53
30	Received from L. Oswald his Bill at one month . .	130·65

EXERCISE 67

Compile Bills Book, and post into the Ledger—

19··		£
Jun 1	Gave my Acceptance at one month to A. Delves	72·63
6	Received from S. Unwin his Bill at three months	170·25
10	Accepted W. Hamnett's Draft at two months	130·50
15	W. Noon accepted my Draft at four months	260·50
22	Drew on B. Sheldon at one month, and he accepted and returned my Draft on the 24th	350·00
26	Gave my Acceptance to W. Wheeldon at one month	88·90
30	Received from B. Connor, A. Steele's Acceptance at two months from 20th June	140·25

EXERCISE 68

Enter into the proper books, post, and balance, drawing out Trial Balance, Trading, Profit and Loss Account, and Balance Sheet. Estimate Stock of Goods unsold on 31st Jan., at £310

19··		£
Jan 1	Commenced Business with cash	1,000·00
2	Paid into Bank	960·00
4	Bought Goods for cheque	150·53
8	Sold Goods for cheque	80·50
12	Paid into Bank	20·00
15	Bought of G. Luke, Goods	200·00
18	Sold Goods to A. Banks	40·25
20	Received of A. Banks, cheque	38·24
	Allowed him discount	2·01
21	Sold Goods to F. Condron	60·00
24	Bought Goods of C. Drain	120·00
28	Gave C. Drain my Acceptance at one month	117·00
	Was allowed discount	3·00
30	Received of F. Condron his Bill at two months	57·00
	Allowed him discount	3·00
31	Paid Trade Expenses by cheque	13·63

CHAPTER XXV

THE MATURITY OF BILLS

In some businesses the transactions in Bills are very few and therefore there is not a sufficient need for a special and expensively ruled Bills Book. In such cases it is usual to make use of the one book that can be used for any transaction, viz. the Journal. In journalizing bill transactions we *debit* the Bills Receivable Account with the bills we *receive*, and *credit* the Bills Payable Account with the bills we *give*, crediting or debiting the personal accounts respectively.

When a Bill Receivable falls due, or, as it is technically called, when it arrives at *maturity*, and we receive *cash* for it, we *debit* the Cash Book with the amount "To Bills Receivable Account," and *credit* the Bills Receivable Account "By Cash." The reason of this will be clear, if we think for a moment. A bill is an undertaking to pay a certain amount at a certain date; when the time arrives, and the money is paid, of course, the person who gave the bill (the undertaking to pay) receives his bill back again. The Bills Receivable Account *gives* (or *sends*) him back his bill, and so the Bills Receivable Account is *creditor*, while the Cash Book, which *receives* the cash for the bill, is *debtor*. If we *debit* the Bills Receivable Account when it *receives* a bill, we must *credit* it when it *gives* or *sends* out a bill.

On the other hand, when a Bill Payable arrives at maturity, and we pay *cash* for the amount of the bill, we *debit* Bills Payable Account with the sum paid, and *credit* the Cash Book which *paid* it. This will be understood when we consider that a bill comes *in* (for, having paid the bill, we receive our written undertaking back again) and cash goes *out*. Besides, if we *credit* the Bills Payable Account when it *gives* a bill, we must *debit* it when the bill comes back, after being paid. When a bill is paid on arriving at *maturity*, it is said to be *honoured* or *retired*.

In the same way, if we *discount* a bill at a banker's, that is, if we receive money for it before it has reached maturity, we *debit* the Cash Book with the *full* amount of the Bill, *crediting* the Cash Book with the discount charged by the banker, this latter being posted to the *debit* of the Bank Charges Account (which is, of course, a *loss* to us); and *credit* the Bills Receivable Account with the *total* amount of the bill, because, when the banker gives us the *money*, we must give him the *bill*.

Now, try to work the following exercises, and if you find any difficulty in them, refer to the explanation just given, and you will find it will give you the assistance you require.

Enter the following transactions into the Books of Original Entry, post into the Ledger, balance and close the accounts; prepare Trial Balance, Trading and Profit and Loss Account, and Balance Sheet.

EXERCISE 69

19..		£
Apr 1	Commenced Business with cash	700·00
2	Bought Goods for cash	300·00
6	Sold to J. Jones, Goods	150·00
9	Received from J. Jones, his Acceptance at one month .	146·25
	Allowed him discount	3·75
12	Sold to G. King, Goods	50·50
14	Bought of M. Rayner, Goods	116·00
16	Gave M. Rayner my Acceptance at two months for .	110·20
	Was allowed discount	5·80
23	Discounted J. Jones's Acceptance—receiving in cash .	144·48
	Discount charged by banker	1·77
30	Paid Trade Expenses	15·00
	Value of Stock on 30th April, £240·50.	

EXERCISE 70

19..		£
May 1	Commenced Business with cash	400·00
3	Bought of C. Bates, Goods	100·50
5	Gave C. Bates my Acceptance at two months for . .	95·48
	Was allowed discount	5·02
8	Sold Goods to H. Clay	50·00
10	Received from H. Clay, Bill at one month for . .	48·75
	Allowed him discount	1·25
12	Bought Goods for cash	20·00
14	Sold Goods for cash	5·50
18	Discounted H. Clay's Bill, receiving cash . . .	48·52
	Discount charged by banker	0·23
21	Sold Goods to H. Jennings	15·75
25	Bought of C. Bates, Goods	70·53
31	Paid Trade Expenses	10·00

Stock of Goods on hand (for Ledger only), £141·53.

QUESTIONS

1. How do you journalize bill transactions?

2. What do you mean by the *maturity* of a bill?

3. What does *honouring* or *retiring* a bill mean?

4. When a bill is matured, and is paid in cash, which account do you *debit*? Which account is credited?

5. When a Bill Payable falls due, and the cash is paid for it, what would be the Journal entry?

6. I discount a bill at the bankers, receiving cash £995, and am charged £5 for the discount. What is the Journal entry?

EXERCISES ON CHAPTER XXV

EXERCISE 71

Enter the following into the proper subsidiary books. Post and balance the accounts; prepare Trial Balance, Trading and Profit and Loss Accounts, and Balance Sheet. Value of Goods on hand on 30th November is £98·50.

19..		£
Nov 1	Commenced Business with cash	1,000·00
2	Bought of Bamber & Co., Goods	300·00
6	Sold to Reed & Sons, Goods	100·00
9	Gave Bamber & Co. my Acceptance at one month .	292·50
	Was allowed discount	7·50
11	Bought of Bamber & Co., Goods	200·00
13	Received of Reed & Sons, Bill of Exchange at two months	97·50
	Allowed them discount	2·50
16	Discounted Reed & Sons' Bill, receiving cash .	97·10
	Was charged discount	0·40
20	Accepted Bamber & Co.'s Draft at one month .	190·00
	Was allowed discount	10·00
23	Sold Goods to W. Mason	290·00
27	W. Mason accepted my Draft at two months . .	282·75
	Allowed him discount	7·25
	Sold Goods for cash	50·00
	Paid Trade Expenses	13·18

EXERCISE 72

Enter into the proper books, post, and balance as before. Make out Trial Balance, Trading and Profit and Loss Accounts, and Balance Sheet.

19..		£
Dec 1	Commenced Business with cash . . .	700·00
	Bought Goods from Renshaw & Sons . .	200·00
4	Sold Goods to Ogden Bros.	50·50
8	Sold Goods for cash	10·53
	Accepted Renshaw & Sons' Draft at one month .	195·00
	Was allowed discount	5·00
10	Bought Goods from Fanning & Sons . .	300·00
14	Gave Fanning & Sons my Acceptance . .	285·00
	Was allowed discount	15·00
16	Sold Goods to Weston & Co. . . .	300·50
18	Weston & Co. accepted my Draft at three months .	292·99
	Allowed them discount	7·51
21	Sold Goods to Weston & Co. . . .	40·00
24	Bought Goods from Renshaw & Sons . .	110·00
28	Sold Goods for cash	15·18
31	Paid Trade Expenses	14·40
	Value of Goods unsold, £236.	

EXERCISE 73

On 31st May, 19.., Samuel Johnson found the state of his affairs to be as follows—

	£		£
He owed A. Roberts .	50·50	Bills Receivable on hand	560·00
„ „ R. Maxwell .	100·00	Cash in hand . .	40·26
Bills Payable . . .	300·00	„ „ Bank . .	750·00
T. Benson owed him .	75·53	Goods on hand . .	960·53
G. Fenton . . .	100·00		

The following were the transactions for the succeeding month, and you are asked to show his position, by means of Balance Sheet, on 30th June—

19..		£
Jun 2	Bill Payable, No. 2, due this day, honoured by Bank .	210·00
6	Drew on G. Fenton, at a month, for amount owing by him	97·50
	Discount allowed to him	2·50
9	Accepted R. Maxwell's Draft at two months . .	95·00
	Was allowed discount .	5·00
	Paid A. Roberts, by cheque	47·98
	Discount allowed	2·52
12	Bought Goods from A. Felder	150·00
16	Sold Goods to G. Fenton	200·00
19	Received from T. Benson, cheque . . .	50·00
23	Bill Receivable, No. 4, due this day, paid into Bank .	350·00
26	Sold Goods, and received payment by cheque . .	375·50
	Bought Goods from R. Maxwell . . .	52·25
30	Paid Trade Expenses by cash	17·13
	Value of Goods unsold, £637.	

CHAPTER XXVI

DISHONOURED BILLS

So far we have assumed that all the Bills of Exchange we have received from others have been duly *honoured*, that is to say, *paid*, when they reached *maturity*, or the date on which they were *due*. Unfortunately, however, this does not always turn out to be the fact, for *acceptors* sometimes fail to pay their Bills of Exchange when due. When a person fails to meet, that is, to pay, a bill at maturity, he is said to have *dishonoured* his bill. It is clear that in such a case he still *owes the money*, and, therefore, must be made *debtor* for the amount. It is obvious, too, that the debtor should at once be written to, acquainting him of the fact that his bill has been dishonoured; and, indeed, this is always done, and the tone of the letter is generally severe, demanding immediate settlement.

It is usual, also, to have the dishonoured bill *noted*. **Noting** a bill is a short memorandum by a public notary, certifying that the bill has been duly presented, and that it was dishonoured. The notary makes a charge for his certificate, and, since this charge is incurred through the debtor's failure to pay the bill promptly, the *noting* expenses are also *debited* to the *debtor*, in addition to the amount of the bill.

When a bill is dishonoured, then, *debit* the *acceptor* of the bill with the amount of the bill *and* the noting expenses; *credit* the Bills Receivable Account with the amount of the bill, and the Cash Book, or the account which *paid* them, with the noting expenses.

It often happens, however, that the person who has failed to meet his bill requests an extension of time in which to pay his debt. If this is agreed to, he may *accept* a *new* bill for the amount of his liability, including the noting charges on the dishonoured bill, and *interest* for the extended time which has been allowed him. In such a case, we should *debit* the person and *credit* the Interest Account with the amount of interest charged; then *debit* the Bills Receivable Account, and *credit* the person with the amount of the new bill. The Interest Account is afterwards transferred to the Profit and Loss Account as a profit.

If, on the other hand, the debtor sent us cash, or a cheque for the amount of the bill he had dishonoured, we should *debit* the cash, or the Bank, and *credit* the sender.

So it will be seen that quite a number of things may happen with a Bill of Exchange. It may be held until it falls due and is paid; it may be discounted, or exchanged for cash, before its maturity, by paying a sum to the discounter for the convenience; it may be paid away in settlement of a debt; it may be *renewed*, by arrangement, that is, the original bill may be given back to the acceptor, who, in return, would give a *new* bill, for an extended period, for the original sum and *interest* for the extra time allowed him for payment; or it *may* be dishonoured, as we have just explained.

If you should find any difficulty in dealing with the cases of dishonoured bills which may be found in succeeding exercises, refer to this chapter for an explanation.

Questions

1. What do you understand by a "dishonoured bill"?

2. When you find you have a customer who has dishonoured his bill, what course would you take? State the Journal entry.

3. Suppose, after you had debited a person who had dishonoured his bill with the amount of the bill and noting expenses, he sends you cash for the total amount, what would be your Journal entry?

4. If, on the other hand, such a person as the one just supposed, sent you a *new* bill for the amount of his old dishonoured bill *and* charges for noting, what Journal entry would you make?

5. State some of the things which may happen with a bill.

EXERCISES ON CHAPTER XXVI

EXERCISE 74

Enter into the Books of Original Entry, post, and balance; make out Trading and Profit and Loss Accounts, and Balance Sheet, valuing Goods unsold at £1,343·50.

19··		£
Feb 1	G. Bell's Assets consisted of—	
	Cash in hand	15·75
	Cash in Bank	1,500·00
	Goods	2,000·00
	Bills Receivable	750·00
	D. Day	15·38
	E. Ellis	45·50
	And his Liabilities were—	
	W. Wise	70·50
	S. Baxter	40·75
	Bills Payable	300·00
	His transactions during the month were as follows—	
2	Received cash for Goods sold	116·83
3	Paid into Bank	100·00
4	H. Paley's Bill, due this day, returned dishonoured	200·00
	Noting charges on same paid by Bank . . .	1·25
6	Received from H. Paley, cash for the amount of his	
	Dishonoured Bill and Noting Charges . .	201·25
8	Sold Goods to E. Ellis	104·50
	Paid into Bank	200·00
10	Paid W. Wise by cheque	66·98
	Was allowed 5 per cent discount . . .	3·52
14	Received from D. Day by cheque	15·38
17	Sold Goods to D. Day	150·00
	E. Ellis accepted Draft at one month . . .	146·25
	Was allowed discount	3·75
21	Sold Goods to A. Morton	250·00
	Sold Good to E. Ellis	110·25
24	Bills Payable honoured by Bank . . .	180·00
	Bought Goods for cash	5·13
28	Paid Trade Expenses by cheque	13·17

EXERCISE 75

Enter in the subsidiary books, post, and balance. Make out Trading, Profit and Loss Accounts, and Balance Sheet.

Henry Naylor's affairs were as follows—

19..				£
Jul 1	ASSETS.	Cash		23·66
		Bank		1,200·53
		Goods		2,600·00
		T. Lever		300·00
		Bills Receivable		716·50
	LIABILITIES.	A. Gaskell		120·75
		L. Tracy		40·53
		Bills Payable		90·00
2	Heard a rumour that T. Lever had failed. (No entry; the rumour may be false.)			
4	Sold Goods to C. Dowell			500·50
6	Accepted A. Gaskell's Draft at one month			117·73
	Was allowed discount			3·02
8	Paid L. Tracy by cheque			20·00
11	C. Dowell accepted Bill at two months			488·49
	Was allowed discount			12·01
16	Sold Goods to D. Ewart			260·00
18	Received cheque from T. Lever			200·00
	Bill Receivable, due this day, dishonoured by the acceptor, F. Rowley			116·50
	Paid Noting Charges on dishonoured bill, by cash			0·75
21	Received cheque from F. Rowley, on account			60·00
26	Sold Goods for cheque			120·53
	Bought Goods of A. Gaskell			59·76
	Settled L. Tracy's Account by cheque, less 5% discount off total amount			
28	Received cash from T. Lever			85·00
	Allowed him discount			15·00
	Paid into Bank			100·00
	Bought Goods for cheque			10·75
31	Paid Trade Charges by cheque			20·89
	Value of Stock unsold, £1,869.			

EXERCISE 76

Record the following transactions, post, and balance, make out Trading and Profit and Loss Accounts, and Balance Sheet, valuing Goods on hand on 31st August at £1,367·53.

19..			£
Aug 1	*Assets—*		
	Cash		5·67
	Bank		1,165·75
	Goods		1,700·00
	Bills Receivable		479·80
	T. Hiles		85·50
	H. Fry		63·75

19..		£
Aug 1	*Liabilities—*	
	E. Lester	120·88
	Bills Payable	314·70
	G. Grant	255·50
3	Bought Goods for cheque	38·99
4	Bill Receivable, accepted by W. Hopkins, and due	
	this day, returned dishonoured	179·50
	Paid Noting Charges on same by cash . . .	0·88
6	Received cash from T. Hiles	50·00
	Paid into Bank	40·00
	Received from W. Hopkins his acceptance at one	
	month, inclusive of Interest and Noting Charges	
	on his dishonoured bill	181·85
8	Sold Goods to H. Fry	100·00
9	Received H. Fry's acceptance at one month . .	159·67
	Allowed him discount	4·08
10	Bill Payable, due this day, met at Bank. . .	200·50
	Sold Goods to C. Quicke	350·00
12	Paid E. Lester by cheque	114·84
	Was allowed discount	6·04
17	Bought Goods of D. Whaite.	75·50
20	Paid Sundry Trade Charges by cheque . .	3·78
22	Bought Goods of E. Lester	56·82
24	Sold Goods for cash	73·50
	Paid into Bank	60·00
26	Received from T. Hiles cheque to settle his Account	
31	Paid Trade Expenses by cheque	25·53

CHAPTER XXVII

CONSIGNMENTS OUTWARDS

MANY business houses have agents abroad, to whom they send goods to be sold on *commission*; that is, they pay the agent a percentage on the prices obtained for the goods, in return for his services in disposing of them. The practice is of mutual advantage to the merchant and to the agent, for it gives the merchant an enlarged area for the disposal of his goods, and affords him the opportunity of utilizing markets which would otherwise be closed to him; while, to the agents it is, of course, an additional source of income.

When a merchant sends out goods under these conditions, it is called a **Consignment Outwards.** Since the agent, to whom the goods are consigned, does not *buy* the goods outright, it is clear that they still belong to the merchant, whose books must show *where* his property is, as, otherwise, the true state of his affairs could not be ascertained. An account must, therefore, be opened in the Ledger for all such transactions, and such an account is called a *Consignment Account.*

A merchant, however, may send consignments to various places, so that it is necessary that the *name of the place* is mentioned in heading the account; as, for example, "Consignment to Sydney," "Consignment to Calcutta," etc.

Furthermore, when a merchant sends out a consignment of goods to an agent, he is anxious to know, when the goods have been sold, whether he has made a profit or sustained a loss. He cannot tell this, unless he keeps a separate account of the consignment, with all that it *costs* him for carriage, commission, etc., and all that he *receives* from the sale of the goods. Therefore, each consignment is *debited* with all that it *costs* in any way, and *credited* with all that it *brings in.* If the whole of the goods consigned are not sold, the goods *unsold* are held as an asset, and will appear as such in the Balance Sheet.

5

When the agent has sold the goods, he sends the merchant a statement, showing how much has been realized on the consignment, together with his charges, etc., and the balance owing to the merchant. Such a document is known as an **Account Sales.** When the agent receives payment for the goods he sold *on the merchant's behalf*, he *owes* this money *to the merchant*, and is, accordingly, *debited* with the amount, while the Consignment Account is *credited*. The Consignment Account is closed by carrying the *balance* to Profit and Loss Account.

One example, however, is worth a great many words; so we will take an example of a consignment, and show exactly the method of treating it.

19..		£
Jan 1	Consigned to Brown & Co., New York, Goods valued at	600·00
3	Paid by cash, Freight, Insurance, and other charges on Consignment	27·78
31	Received from Brown & Co., New York, Account Sales, showing that Consignment has realized *net* . .	695·78

The following would be the Journal entries for these transactions—

19..			£	£
Jan 1	Consignment to New York . *Dr.*		600·00	
	To Goods on Consignment .			600·00
31	Brown & Co. . . . *Dr.*		695·78	
	To Consignment to New York .			695·78

	CASH BOOK			*Cr.*
19..				£
Jan 3	By Consignment to New York . .			27·78

These items would be posted to the Ledger, and the Consignment Account closed, as follows—

Dr.	CONSIGNMENT TO NEW YORK		Cr.
19..		£	19..		£

Dr.   CONSIGNMENT TO NEW YORK   Cr.

		£			£
Jan 1	To Goods	600·00	Jan 31	By Brown & Co.	695·78
3	Cash	27·78			
31	Balance transferred to Profit & Loss	68·00			
		695·78			695·78

Dr.   GOODS ON CONSIGNMENT ACCOUNT   Cr.

					£
			Jan 1	By Consignment to N.Y.	600·00

Dr.   BROWN & CO., NEW YORK   Cr.

		£		
Jan 31	To Consignment	695·78		

Dr.   PROFIT AND LOSS ACCOUNT   Cr.

					£
			Jan 31	By Transfer from Consignment to N.Y.	68·00

It will be seen that, in the example given, there has been a profit of £68 on the consignment. Brown & Co. have been *debited* with the net amount they received for the goods, and when they send the money to the merchant, they will be *credited*.

QUESTIONS

1. What is a Consignment Outwards?
2. What advantages does it give to a merchant?

3. How can a merchant tell whether he has lost or gained on a Consignment?

4. What is an Account Sales?

5. If you had consigned goods to Melbourne, and your agent sent you an Account Sales showing the amount realized on the consignment, what entry would you make in your books?

6. How is a Consignment Account closed?

EXERCISES ON CHAPTER XXVII

EXERCISE 77

James White, on 30th November, 19.., found his Balance Sheet to show the following—

Assets	£	Liabilities	£
Cash in hand	20·53	E. Morris	90·00
Cash in Bank	850·50	W. Anderson	30·50
Goods in hand	900·00	Bills Payable	150·00
H. Dacre	45·13		
F. Booth	60·27		
Bills Receivable	270·00		

During December his transactions were as follows—

19..		£
Dec 1	Bill Receivable, No. 1, discounted at Bank	
	Amount received in cash	169·25
	Discount charged	0·75
2	Bought Goods for cheque	150·00
4	Sold Goods to H. Dacre	210·50
8	Received from F. Booth, cheque	58·76
	Allowed him discount	1·51
12	Accepted E. Morris's Draft at one month	85·50
	Was allowed discount	4·50
15	Sold Goods for cash	300·00
	Paid into Bank	310·00
16	Sold Goods to F. Booth	85·18
19	H. Dacre accepted Bill at three months	249·24
	Was allowed discount	6·39
23	Bill Payable, No. 4, honoured by Bank	150·00
25	Bought Goods from E. Morris	96·80
28	Sold Goods for cheque	25·73
31	Paid Trade Expenses by cheque	19·16
	Value of stock on hand (for Ledger only), £580.	

Show his position on 31st December by Balance Sheet.

EXERCISE 78

On 31st January, 19.., the position of Arthur Webb's affairs was as follows—

		£
He had Cash in hand	. . . .	35·82
,, ,, Bank	. . . .	1,150·50
,, Goods	. . . .	1,760·53
,, Bills Receivable	. . . .	592·00
Owing by B. Bray	. . . .	110·00
,, E. Etchells	. . . .	67·50
He owed to H. Cane	. . . .	85·75
,, C. Heane	. . . .	250·50
,, Bills Payable	. . . .	475·83

His transactions during February were as follows; and you are required to enter them into the proper books, post, and balance the same, making out Trading and Profit and Loss Accounts, and Balance Sheet. Estimate Goods unsold at end of month at £1,464.

19..		£
Feb 2	Bought Goods and paid for same by cheque .	160·53
	Shipping on consignment to W. Finch, Rouen, Goods	120·75
	Paid by cheque, Sundry Charges, Freight, etc., on consignment	16·26
4	Sold to B. Bray, Goods	90·00
	Bills Payable, due this day, honoured by Bank . .	175·83
6	Drew on B. Bray, at two months' date . . .	190·00
	Allowed him discount	10·00
8	Received from E. Etchells, cash	64·12
	And allowed him discount	3·38
12	Paid into Bank	50·00
15	Bills Receivable due this day, received by Bank .	392·00
	Paid H. Cane by cheque	81·46
	Was allowed discount	4·29
17	Bills Receivable No. 2, due this day, and which was accepted by K. Hilton returned dishonoured . .	100·00
	Paid by cash, noting charges on dishonoured bill .	0·75
21	Received from K. Hilton, new bill at three months, including noting charges and interest . . .	102·03
24	Sold Goods to B. Bray	125·75
	Sold Goods to E. Etchells	170·00
26	Received Account Sales from W. Finch, Rouen, showing that Consignments, after deducting commission, etc., realized	156·85
28	Paid Trade Expenses by cheque	23·29

EXERCISE 79

Enter into the books, post, and balance. Open *separate* accounts for Port, Sherry, and Brandy. On 1st September, 19.., the books of S. Pyper showed the following balances—

Assets	£	Liabilities	£
Cash in hand	30·53	G. Cook	250·00
Bank	2,500·00	H. Reid	120·50
Port Wine	350·00	Bills Payable (due 9th	
Sherry	350·00	Sept.)	750·00
Brandy	1,600·00		
J. Russell	500·50		
Bills Rec.	500·00		

19..		£
Sep 2	Sold to Ashton & Co., Port Wine for	120·00
3	Paid in Cash, Dock Charges on Port sold to Ashton & Co.	4·50
6	Consigned to Peters & Sons, Melbourne, to be sold on Commission, on S. Pyper's account and risk, Brandy	1,000·00
7	Paid for Insurance, Dock Charges, etc., on Consignment of Brandy, by cheque	45·53
9	Bill Payable, due this day, duly honoured by Bank	750·00
12	Sold to A. Moores, Sherry Wine	200·50
	Received cheque from J. Russell	300·00
14	Paid by Cash, Dock Charges on Sherry Wine sold to A. Moores	3·63
16	Bought Sherry Wine for cheque	70·75
	Bill Receivable, due this day, received by Bank	350·00
18	Accepted G. Cook's Bill at one month for	242·50
	Was allowed discount	7·50
21	J. Russell, having been declared bankrupt, pays in cash a composition of 75p in the £.	
	Paid into Bank	150·00
	Sold Brandy to B. Drighton	300·00
	Paid Dock Charges on same, cash	3·23
	Bought Brandy from H. Reid	124·50
23	Accepted H. Reid's Bill at one month, in payment of of his account, less 5% discount	
28	Sold for cash, Sherry Wine	111·75
	Sold for cash, Port Wine	56·50
	Sold for cash, Brandy	98·75
29	Paid by cash, Dock Charges on Cash Sales yesterday, as follows—	
	Sherry Wine, £4·53; Port, £2·60; Brandy, £6·78.	
	Paid Trade Expenses by cash	36·26
	Paid into Bank	230·00
30	Stocks on hand: Port, £201; Sherry, £140; Brandy, £475.	

Note. Since it is desired to know the profit or loss on *each* account, it will be necessary to *debit* each account with what it *costs* in the way of dock charges, etc. The Consignment will appear as an Asset in the Balance Sheet.

EXERCISE 80

Enter into the proper books, post, and balance, valuing Stock on hand on 31st October at £827.

19..		£
Oct 1	*Assets*—	
	Cash	15·63
	Bank	500·53
	Goods	1,750·00
	B. Best	49·50
	Liabilities—	
	T. Tristam	97·75
	W. Shann	120·50
	Bills Payable	175·50
	Sold Goods to R. Scott	50·83
2	Shipped on Consignment to F. Shein, Boston, Goods valued at	760·53
3	Paid by cheque, Freight and Insurance on Consignment to Boston	31·61
5	Sold Goods for cash	63·65
	Paid into Bank	50·00
	Bill Payable, honoured by Bank	175·50
8	Received from B. Best, cheque	49·50
	Paid T. Tristam by cheque	92·86
	Was allowed discount	4·89
12	Bought Goods of W. Shann	79·50
14	Accepted W. Shann's Draft at one month to settle	195·00
	Was allowed 2½% discount	5·00
16	Sold Goods to B. Best	210·00
	Sold Goods to D. Somers	75·88
23	Bought Goods of T. Tristam	48·93
26	Paid Sundry Trade Charges, cash	3·83
31	Received Account Sales from F. Shein, showing net proceeds of Consignment to be	827·50
	Paid Trade Expenses by cheque	24·74

EXERCISE 81

From the following Balance Sheet, and the succeeding particulars show the position of Abraham Bell on 31st

January, 19... The transactions are to be entered into the proper books and posted, Trial Balance drawn out, the accounts closed, and a Balance Sheet presented at end of month—

BALANCE SHEET OF ABRAHAM BELL, ON 31ST DECEMBER, 19..

Liabilities	£	Assets	£
M. Bond	55·53	Cash in hand	10·00
T. Lander	72·75	Cash in Bank	500·00
Balance (Capital)	1,746·24	Goods in hand	810·50
		Bills Receivable	370·38
		W. Trainer	60·25
		S. Slater	30·13
		A. Strong	93·26
	1,874·52		1,874·52

19..		£
Jan 1	A. Strong accepted Bill at two months	88·60
	Was allowed discount	4·66
4	Received cheque from W. Trainer	58·74
	Allowed him discount	1·51
6	Sold Goods to S. Slater	320·25
8	Bought Goods from M. Bond	160·48
10	Bills Receivable, No. 3, paid into Bank	170·38
11	Accepted M. Bond's Draft at one month	205·20
	Was allowed discount	10·80
15	Sold Goods for cheque	45·46
	S. Slater accepted Draft at one month	341·61
	Was allowed discount	8·76
18	Bought Goods for cheque	56·80
22	Sold Goods to A. Strong	120·00
	Paid T. Lander, by cheque	69·11
	Was allowed discount	3·64
24	Bought Goods of T. Lander	45·53
26	Sold Goods to W. Trainer	15·00
31	Paid Trade Expenses, by cheque	23·52
	Value of Stock on hand, £610.	

CHAPTER XXVIII

CONSIGNMENTS INWARDS

It will readily be understood that a merchant may not only consign goods to agents abroad, but *he* may, in turn, act as agent for other merchants. In other words, he may not only consign goods himself, but he may *receive* consignments from others. When *he* receives a consignment of goods, to be sold on commission, the consignment is known as a **Consignment Inwards**. Such a case requires rather different treatment from a Consignment Outwards.

When we receive a Consignment Inwards, beyond acknowledging the receipt of the goods to the senders, we take no further action, as far as the *books* are concerned. We should, of course, busy ourselves to find customers for the goods. But immediately we *pay* anything on account of the goods, in the way of carriage, for instance, or as soon as we *sell* the goods, or any part of them, *then a transaction* has taken place, which must be recorded in our books.

When, therefore, we pay anything on account of a Consignment Inwards, we *debit* the Consignor, or sender of the goods, and *credit* Cash or Bank, as the case may be; when we sell the goods, or part of them, we *debit* the *buyer*, and *credit* the *consignor*; when we receive payment for goods which formed part (or the whole) of the Consignment Inwards, we *debit* Cash, or the Bank, or Bills Receivable, according as the payment is made in the form of cash, cheque, or a bill, and we *credit* the payer; when the goods are all sold, we *debit* the Consignor's Account with our commission, and *credit* Commission Account; finally, we submit an Account Sales, showing how much the Consignment realized, what it cost for carriage, storage, commission, etc., and how much is the balance owing to the consignor of the goods. When the amount represented by the balance is sent to the consignor, he is, of course, *debited* with the amount, while the paying account, Cash, Bank, or Bills Payable, is *credited*.

This is a long statement, you will think; but, if you go over it once more, you will see that it follows the order of events. Just try it, and you will find there is (1) the receipt of the Consignment; (2) a probable payment on account of it; (3) a sale of the goods, or part of them; (4) a receipt in payment of the goods sold; (5) a charging (debiting) of the Consignor's Account for our trouble in receiving and selling the goods; (6) a presentation of a statement showing how much the goods have realized; and (7) a payment by us to the consignor of the balance due to him.

Let us, however, take an example to illustrate this long explanation.

19..		£
Feb 1	Received from Jenner & Co. on Consignment, to be sold on their account, and at their risk, Goods valued	1,250·00
2	Paid by cheque, dock charges, etc., on above .	5·88
6	Sold Entwistle & Sons, part of above Consignment	650·00
13	Received from Entwistle & Sons, cheque .	650·00
15	Sold to D. Fennel, remainder of Jenner & Co.'s Consignment	780·00
16	Received from D. Fennel, cheque . .	780·00
	Paid by cash, for Storage of Jenner & Co's Consignment	1·12
	Our Commission on Jenner & Co.'s Consignment is	35·75
27	Accepted Jenner & Co.'s Draft at one month .	1,387·25

The Journal entries for these transactions are as follows—

19..			Dr.	Cr.
			£	£
Feb 1	No entry. Simply acknowledge receipt of goods			
6	Entwistle & Sons .	Dr.	650·00	
	To Jenner & Co.	.		650·00
15	D. Fennel .	Dr.	780·00	
	To Jenner & Co.	.		780·00
16	Jenner & Co. .	Dr.	35·75	
	To Commission .	.		35·75
27	Jenner & Co. .	Dr.	1,387·25	
	To Bills Payable	.		1,387·25

Dr.   CASH BOOK   Cr.

		CASH	BANK				CASH	BANK
19.. Feb 13	To Entwistle & Sons		£ 650·00	19.. Feb 2	By Jenner & Co.		£	£
16	D. Fennel		780·00	16	Jenner & Co.		1·12	5·88

QUESTIONS

1 How many kinds of Consignments are there?

2. What is a "Consignment Inwards"?

3. What would you do on receiving Goods on Consignment?

4. Suppose you paid something on account of the Consignment?

5. What entry would you make if you sold part of the Goods?

6. Whose account would you debit with your commission for selling the Goods? Which account would be credited?

7. When the owner of a business withdraws money for his private purposes, what entry would you make? Give your reasons for this.

EXERCISES ON CHAPTER XXVIII
EXERCISE 82

On 1st March, 19.., E. Pooley commenced business with a Capital of £5,000. Enter into the proper books the transactions which are given, post, and balance the Ledger, and prepare a Trial Balance and Balance Sheet.

19..		£
Mar 1	Paid into Bank	4,500·00
	Bought of Kennedy & Co., Goods	2,700·00
3	Accepted Kennedy & Co.'s Draft at one month	2,632·50
	Was allowed as discount	67·50
7	Received from De Montfort & Co., Paris, on Consignment, to be sold on their account and risk, Goods valued	1,000·00
8	Paid, by cheque, sundry charges on above Consignment	15·82
10	Sold Goods to Klein & Sons	1,500·00

19..		£
Mar 4	Sold Goods for cash	250·00
	Paid into Bank	610·00
16	Sold the whole of De Montfort's Consignment to D. Jewsbury	1,150·00
18	Received cheque from D. Jewsbury . .	1,150·00
20	Bought of Webster & Sons, Goods . .	350·53
	Forwarded Bill of Exchange at sight to De Montfort & Co., in settlement	1,105·43
	Charged for Commission	28·75
22	Mr. Pooley took cash for his private expenses .	50·00
27	Received from Klein & Sons, Bill of Exchange at two months for	1,462·50
	Allowed them discount	37·50
	Bought of Kennedy & Co., Goods . .	300·00
28	Sold to Klein & Sons, Goods . . .	450·00
31	Paid Trade Expenses by cash . . .	30·00
	Stock of Goods unsold, £1,320.	

Note. In entering the item on 22nd March, "Mr. Pooley took cash for his private expenses," *debit* E. Pooley's Capital Account, and *credit* Cash Book. When E. Pooley brought cash *into* the business he was *credited*, as in the instance on the 1st March; when he takes cash *out* of the business for his *private* expenses, he must be *debited*, since it reduces the Capital he has invested in the business. Moreover, E. Pooley is the *receiver* on this occasion, and the receiver is *debtor*.

EXERCISE 83

Enter into the proper books, post, and balance the following—

19..		£
Nov 1	Commenced Business with cash . . .	1,000·00
	Paid into Bank	900·00
2	Bought Goods from Prince & Co. . .	350·50
5	Received from Brown & Son, Boston, U.S.A., to be sold on their account and risk, Goods . .	245·50
6	Paid Sundry Charges on Consignment by cash .	15·51
8	Accepted Prince & Co.'s Bill at one month for .	332·98
	Was allowed discount	17·53
	Sold Goods for cash	100·00
10	Paid into Bank	120·00
	Sold part of Brown & Son's Consignment to F. Lowe for cash*	190·00

19..		£
Nov 10	Paid into Bank	230·00
15	Bought Goods of H. Kirk	200·00
17	Sold remainder of Brown & Son's Consignment to	
	L. Eckersley for cheque*.	95·50
	Debit Brown & Son, for commission . .	14·28
24	Sold Goods for cheque	210·98
31	Paid Trade Expenses by cash	17·25
	Stock of Goods unsold, £269.	

*Note. There is no need to open accounts for F. Lowe
or L. Eckersley. As the goods were paid for at once, the
receiving accounts, Cash and Bank, may be debited with the
respective amounts.

EXERCISE 84

Enter into the proper books, post, and balance.

19..		£
Dec 1	*Assets—*	
	Cash	10·53
	Bank	355·88
	Goods	500·00
	Bills Receivable	425·50
	Liabilities—	
	P. Bibby	30·88
	W. Yates	64·50
	T. Garnett	5·25
2	Settled Yate's Account by cheque, less 5% discount .	
	Sold Goods to J. Riggs	140·50
5	Received from Barnett Bros., on Consignment, Goods	
	valued	300·75
9	Bill Receivable, due this day, received by Bank .	125·50
10	Sold to E. Grime the whole of Consignment from	
	Barnett Bros.	360·25
14	Paid by cheque, Freight and other charges on Barrett's	
	Consignment	19·63
	Received from J. Riggs, cheque	50·00
	Paid T. Garnett, cash	5·25
17	Received from E. Grime, cheque . . .	360·25
24	Bought Goods of W. Yates	78·91
31	Forwarded to Barnett Bros., Bill at Sight for .	331·63
	Charging as Commission on Consignment. .	9·00
	Sold Goods for cheque	80·75
	Paid Trade Expenses by cheque . . .	16·80
	Value of Stock, £379.	

EXERCISE 85

Enter in the subsidiary books, post, and balance the following transactions. Present a Balance Sheet on 28th February. At the end of January, 19.., Edward Dann's books showed the following—

19..		£
Jan 31	*Assets—*	
	Cash in hand	30·78
	Cash in Bank	300·53
	Goods in hand	1,200·00
	A. Wilson	60·83
	B. Makin	40·18
	Bills Receivable	350·00
	Liabilities—	
	Bills Payable	400·00
	B. Barnes	65·75
Feb 1	Sold Goods for cash	150·50
5	Paid B. Barnes, cash	62·46
	Was allowed discount	3·29
	Paid into Bank, cash	90·00
8	Received from A. Wilson, cheque . . .	50·00
10	Received cheque for Goods sold . . .	120·53
12	Sold Goods to B. Makin	80·83
14	B. Makin accepted Draft at one month . .	117·98
	Was allowed discount	3·03
17	Bill Payable, honoured by Bank . . .	200·00
19	Discounted B. Makin's Draft, receiving cash .	117·58
	Was charged for discounting . . .	0·40
	Paid into Bank . . . . . —	140·00
24	Bought Goods for cheque	27·50
26	Sold Goods for cheque	90·78
28	Paid Trade Expenses, by cheque . . .	11·38
	Stock in hand	837·53

CHAPTER XXIX

PARTNERSHIP ACCOUNTS

So far, we have considered only the methods of keeping the books of businesses belonging, in each case, to *one* person. The student will, doubtless, be aware of many instances of businesses in which *several* persons are interested; where two or more persons own the business, which is carried on as a company, as "John Brown & Co."; or "James and Henry Blake," etc.

Where such is the case, it is necessary to keep a separate Capital Account for *each* partner, in order to show the amount each has invested in the business. So as to keep a partner's Capital Account clear from a number of entries of details' it is usual to open, in addition, a **"Drawings Account"** or **"Current Account"** for each partner. This account is *debited* with any amount which may be withdrawn from the business, together with interest on such amount, and, also, with the partner's share of any losses which may be sustained by the firm; it is *credited* with interest on the partner's capital, and also with his share of the business profits. The Drawings Account or Current Account balance is carried to the Balance Sheet.

The following example will make the method clear—

On 1st April, 19.., James Kenyon and Edwin Hall commenced business in partnership, each contributing £2,500 towards the firm's capital. The partners are to receive interest on their capital at the rate of 5 per cent per annum, and are to be charged a similar rate on any sums withdrawn from the business. Profit or losses to be equally divided.

The capital contributed would be entered in the Cash Book "To J. Kenyon, Capital Account £2,500" and "To E. Hall, Capital Account £2,500." If J. Kenyon's drawings were £35, drawn on 10th April, and E. Hall's £50, drawn on 23rd April, the interest chargeable would be J. Kenyon 10p (5 per cent on £35 for two-thirds months) and E. Hall 5p (5 per cent on £50 for one quarter month). The interest on each partner's capital for one month at 5 per cent is £10·42. The following entries will show how these items are journalized.

			Dr.	Cr.
			£	£
19.. Apr 30	Interest a/c . . . . . Dr.		10·42	
	To J. Kenyon (Drawings a/c) . .			10·42
	Interest a/c . . . . . Dr.		10·42	
	To E. Hall (Drawings a/c) . .			10·42
	J. Kenyon (Drawings a/c) . . Dr.		0·10	
	To Interest a/c			0·10
	E Hall (Drawings a/c) . . Dr.		0·05	
	To Interest a/c			0·05
			20·99	20·99

EXERCISE 86

Including the above example, enter the following transactions into the proper subsidiary books, post and balance, dividing the balance of Profit and Loss Account equally between the two partners. Carry each partner's share to his Current Account. Make up Trading and Profit and Loss Accounts, and submit a Balance Sheet.

19..		£
Apr 1	Paid into Bank	4,950·00
3	Bought Goods of Mawson Bros. . . .	1,000·00
5	Sold Goods for cash	50·00
6	Accepted Mawson Bros.' Draft at one month .	950·00
	Was allowed discount	50·00
8	Sold Goods to J. Roddy	250·00
10	J. Kenyon withdrew for private purposes, cash .	35·00
	Bought Goods of Condron & Co. . . .	750·50
12	Sold Goods to J. Beech	200·00
17	Received from J. Roddy, cheque . . .	150·00
20	Sold Goods to W. Lewis	300·00
22	W. Lewis accepted Bill at two months for .	292·50
	Was allowed discount	7·50

19..		£
Apr 23	E. Hall's private expenses paid by cheque . .	50·00
26	Sold Goods and received payment by cheque. .	95·53
	Received from J. Roddy, cheque for . .	93·75
	Allowed him discount	6·25
28	Bought Goods for cash	10·00
	Paid into Bank	30·00
30	Paid Trade Expenses, by cheque	21·98
	Credit J. Kenyon with interest on Capital . .	10·42
	Debit J. Kenyon with interest on Drawings . .	0·10
	Credit E. Hall with interest on Capital . . .	10·42
	Debit E. Hall with interest on Drawings . .	0·05
	Stock of Goods unsold, £954.	

QUESTIONS

1. In the case of a partnership how many Capital Accounts would you require?

2. What other account would you open for each partner?

3. How would you close the Drawings Account?

4. What is the advantage of having a Drawings Account in addition to the Capital Account of each partner?

5. To what account would you carry the balance of Profit and Loss?

EXERCISES ON CHAPTER XXIX
EXERCISE 87

Enter the following transactions in appropriate books, Post to Ledger, and prepare Trial Balance, Trading, Profit and Loss Account, and Balance Sheet.

Open a separate Capital Account for each partner.

BALANCE SHEET, 31ST AUGUST, 19..

Liabilities		£	Assets		£
F. Gray . . .		31·86	Cash in hand . .		1,606·36
G. Fail . . .		300·00	Goods in Stock . .		2,210·00
F. Harper . .		1,000·00	B. Birch . . .		300·00
J. Carter (Capital)		2,000·00	D. Dean . . .		170·50
A. Spur ,,		1,000·00	E. Gaul . . .		45·00
		4,331·86			4,331·86

			£
19..			
Sep 1	Received from B. Birch, cash		200·00
3	Sold Goods to E. Gaul		99·50
5	Bought Goods of G. Fail		50·00
8	Sold Goods for cash		163·68
12	Received from D. Dean, cash to settle his Account, *less* 5% discount		
16	Paid G. Fail, by cash		285·00
	Discount allowed		15·00
19	Sold Goods for cash		72·60
23	Received from E. Gaul, cash		43·88
	Allowed him discount		1·12
27	Sold Goods to D. Dean		348·50
	Paid Travelling Expenses		18·48
29	Sold Goods for cash		163·50
30	Paid F. Harper, by cash		500·00
	Paid Trade Expenses, by cash . . .		29·33
	Stock of Goods on hand		1,580·00

Divide Profit or Loss as follows: Two-thirds to J. Carter; one-third to A. Spurr.

EXERCISE 88

James and Henry Lever are in partnership, and on 31st January, 19.., their Balance Sheet is as follows—

Liabilities		£	*Assets*		£
F. Joyce . . .		90·75	Cash in hand . . .		40·51
Bills Payable . . .		330·53	Cash in Bank . . .		1,550·75
J. Lever (Capital) . .		1,825·49	Goods		2,000·00
H. Lever (Capital) .		1,825·49	S. Simons . . .		100·00
			Bills Receivable . .		380·90
		4,072·26			4,072·26

The Profit or Loss is to be divided equally.

			£
19..			
Feb 1	Bill Receivable, due this day, accepted by A. Robson, dishonoured		180·00
	Noting Charges paid by cash		1·10
2	Consigned to Blake & Sons, Baltimore, to be sold on account and risk of J. & H. Lever, Goods . .		475·50
3	Received from A. Robson, cheque in payment of his Bill and Noting Charges		181·10

19..		£
Feb 3	Bought Goods of Jones & Co.	135·00
	Paid Freight and Insurance on Consignment, by cheque	23·68
5	Sold Goods to S. Simons	340·00
	Accepted Jones & Co's Bill at two months . .	131·63
	Being allowed discount	3·37
10	A. Beard's bill, due this day, received at Bank .	200·90
14	James Lever withdrew cash for Private Expenses .	30·00
	S. Simons accepted Bill at one month . .	423·50
	Was allowed discount	16·50
18	Sold Goods for cheque	75·78
	Bill Payable honoured by Bank . . .	230·53
	Bought Goods of F. Joyce . . .	56·80
24	Paid F. Joyce by cheque	88·48
	Was allowed discount	2·27
26	Sold Goods to P. Kirby	48·81
27	Received Account Sales from Blake & Sons, Baltimore,	
	showing net proceeds of consignment to be .	560·00
	And their Bill at fourteen days for . . .	560·00
28	Paid Trade Expenses by cheque . . .	31·08
	Debit James Lever with interest on Drawings .	0·06
	Credit James Lever with interest on Capital .	7·60
	Credit Henry Lever with interest on Capital .	7·60
	Stock unsold, £1,301.	

APPENDIX

EXAMINATION PAPERS

Union of Educational Institutions

Book-keeping: S1

1. From the following items construct the Balance Sheet of L. Redfern as on 31st December—

	£
Capital as at 1st January	200·00
Motor Vans as at 31st December	220·00
Cash at Bank as at 31st December	70·00
Profit for the year	300·00
Land and Buildings as at 31st December . . .	410·00
Drawings for the year	150·00
Stock of Goods, 31st December	230·00
Loan from A. Herbert	400·00
Debtors as at 31st December	200·00
Sundry Creditors as at 31st December . . .	380·00

2. From the following particulars, draw up the Capital Account of J. Owen as it would appear in his books for the year. Balance it off as on the 31st December, and bring down the balance—

	£
Capital as at 1st January	416·25
Profit for the year was	314·28
On 15th October J. Owen paid in additional Capital . .	500·00
During the year J. Owen drew out of the business for private expenses	250·00
On 31st December interest on Capital was allowed . .	22·00

3. On 1st March, a cheque for £20 was handed to the petty cashier to pay petty cash expenses for the month, which were as follows—

19..			£
Mar 1	Postage Stamps		2·00
3	Carriage		0·24
4	Bus Fares		0·04
5	Shorthand Note Books		0·53
6	Postage Stamps		1·00
8	Fare to London		1·25
9	Sundry Trade Expenses		0·51

19..											£
Mar 11	Pencils	.	.	.	.	.	.	.	.	.	0·13
14	Trunk Call	.	.	.	.	.	.	.	.	.	0·38
16	Envelopes	.	.	.	.	.	.	.	.	.	0·25
18	Stationery	.	.	.	.	.	.	.	.	.	0·88
31	Carriage	.	.	.	.	.	.	.	.	.	0·27

Rule a Petty Cash Book in analysis form, with five analysis columns, headed Postages and Telephone, Carriage, Travelling Expenses, Stationery, and Sundry Trade Expenses respectively. Enter the foregoing items and close the book as on 31st March, showing clearly the balance of cash in hand.

4. The following Trial Balance was extracted from the books of B. Gwilliams as at the 31st December—

	£	£
B. Gwilliams's Capital Account, 1st January .		2,500
Purchases	2,100	
Rent and Rates	40	
Drawings	260	
Sales		4,926
Stock, 1st January	1,250	
Bad Debts	50	
Motor Vans	855	
Purchases Returns		174
Discounts Allowed	83	
Sales Returns	45	
Heating and Lighting	59	
Wages	2,141	
Discount Received		45
Sundry Debtors	462	
Insurance	67	
Cash at Bank	838	
Sundry Creditors		755
Sundry Trade Expenses	150	
	8,400	8,400

The Stock on 31st December was £736. You are required to prepare Trading, Profit and Loss Account for the year, and Balance Sheet as on 31st December.

5. Give the Journal entries necessary to record the following facts in the books of I. Markham, a manufacturer—

19..
Jan 1   I. Markham commenced business with Cash in hand, £36; Cash at Bank, £141; Plant and Machinery, £180; and Stock, value £200.

19..
Jan 28   Bought Plant and Machinery on credit from Speed & Co.,
         Ltd., value £130.
Mar 3   A debt for £25 owing by B. Sykes proves worthless.
    10   The Plant and Machinery purchased on credit from Speed & Co.
         was returned as not being according to specification.
    31   £25 interest on Capital to be allowed.

6. Define any five of the following terms—

Debit Note, Credit Note, Trial Balance, Balance Sheet, Current Account,
Nominal Account, Discount Received, Bank Pass Book, Error of Principle,
Compensating Error.

UNION OF LANCASHIRE AND CHESHIRE INSTITUTES,
FIRST YEAR

1. Give the Journal entries necessary to correct the following errors—

19..
Jan 6   £15·21 cash received from H. Hughes has been posted to the
         credit of T. Hughes's Account.
    18   New machinery, costing £30, has been debited to Machinery
         Repairs Account.
    30   Private expenses of £6·63 have been posted to Office Expenses
         Account.

2. A. Bee sold goods £100 to J. Jackson on the 22nd
December. Jackson subsequently became bankrupt, and the
following 14th March A. Bee received a dividend of 17p
in the £ in respect of this account. On the 31st March the
balance was written off as a bad debt. Show J. Jackson's
Account in A. Bee's Ledger.

3. The following accounts appear in the books of a trader:
Plant, J. Brown (a debtor), Wages, Carriage Outwards, Discounts Received, L. Smith (a creditor), Sales, Returns Inwards.

Classify these into Personal, Real, and Nominal Accounts,
and state on which side of the Ledger the balance of the
accounts would appear.

4. What is the difference between an invoice and a statement? Give an example of a credit note, and state when
such a form is used.

5. Open the books of L. Thompson, a pottery dealer, whose
position on the 1st March was as follows—

	£		£
Sundry Creditors—		Premises . . .	1,000·00
J. Wood . .	110·76	Office Furniture .	15·00
H. Bird . .	56·76	Stock . . .	400·00
Bill Payable (due 16th		Sundry Debtors—	
March) . .	240·00	B. Smith . .	199·81
Capital . . .	1,800·00	L. Leek . . .	201·75
		Bill Receivable (due	
		3rd April) .	78·00
		Cash at Bank . .	300·46
		Cash in hand . .	12·50
	2,207·52		2,207·52

Enter the following transactions in the proper subsidiary books, and post to the Ledger. Balance the Ledger, bring down the balances, and extract a Trial Balance as at 17th March.

19..		£	£
Mar 1	Sold on credit to B. Smith 6 dozen tea sets at £6 per dozen, *less* 10 per cent trade discount.		
3	Paid J. Wood by cheque in full settlement .		106·00
	Cash Sales		14·16
	Paid Wages by cash . . .		16·37
	Drew cash for private purposes .		5·00
6	Bought on credit from H. Bird 5 dozen dinner sets at £36 per dozen, 1 dozen dishes at 25p each; all subject to 10 per cent trade discount.		
	B. Smith returned 1 dozen of tea sets sold to him on the 1st instant.		
10	Cash Sales for week		91·16
	Paid Wages by cash . . .		18·16
	Drew cash for Private Purposes . .		5·00
12	Paid cash to Bank		60·00
13	L. Leek paid his account by cheque . .	199·00	
	Allowed him discount . . .	2·75	
			201·75
14	Paid cheque to bank		199·00
16	Bank paid bill payable due this day . .		240·00
	Drew cheque for private purposes . .		15·00
17	Bought by cheque additional office furniture		15·00

Note. No Trading and Profit and Loss Accounts or Balance Sheet are required.

6. From the following Trial Balance of D. Dunn, a manufacturer, prepare Trading and Profit and Loss Accounts for the year ended 31st January and a Balance Sheet as at that date.

The stock on hand at 31st January was valued at £584.

TRIAL BALANCE AT 31ST JANUARY

	£	£
Purchases	3,176	
D. Dunn—		
Capital		1,000
Carriage Inwards	51	
Trade Expenses	311	
Wages	450	
Sales		5,103
Sundry Debtors and Creditors	461	323
Sales Returns	31	
Plant and Machinery	457	
Bad Debts	16	
Discounts	71	14
Postages and Telephone	15	
D. Dunn—		
Drawings	312	
Stock—		
At beginning of year	761	
Cash at Bank	312	
Cash in hand	16	
	6,440	6,440

BUSINESS TERMS AND ABBREVIATIONS

THE following abbreviations and terms will be found useful to the student. A very extensive list of business terms in general use, with equivalents in French, German, Spanish, and Italian, is given in *Pitman's Business Terms, Phrases and Abbreviations*.

Acceptance. When a draft or bill has been presented to the *drawee*, and *signed* or *accepted* by him, it is called an *Acceptance*. The bill is said to be presented for *acceptance*.

Acceptor. The person who *accepts* a bill; the drawee; the person who will have to *pay* the amount.

Account Sales. A statement showing the proceeds of a consignment, with the agent's commission, expenses paid on the goods, etc.

Ad valorem. According to value.

Advice. A written communication wherein one person informs another of something done, or about to be done, on his account.

Amortization. The extinction or reduction of a debt by means of a sinking fund.

Assets. Debts owing to, and property belonging to a person or firm.

Audit. To examine accounts by reference to vouchers and testify as to their correctness.

Auditor. A person appointed to examine and verify accounts of a government, corporation, or firm.

Auxiliary. A name applied to such books as are not posted from, but which are kept as aids to principal books.

Average. (1) A medium time for the payment, in one sum, of several sums due at different times. This is called "Equation of Payments." (2) In shipping, a term signifying adjustment of proportion of loss sustained by insurers.

General Average. The amount charged, *ad valorem*, on the owners of a ship, of its cargo and freight, to cover the loss incurred when *part* of the cargo has been sacrificed, in a storm, or other loss or expense has been incurred, *for the general safety of ship and cargo*. This risk is covered by an ordinary insurance policy.

Particular Average. Partial damage to ship or cargo, resulting from the common perils of the sea and *not affecting the general safety*. Such loss is borne by the insurer or owner.

Free of Particular Average. When the policy of insurance contains this clause, the underwriters are not liable for particular average. If, however, the ship is "stranded, sunk, burnt, on fire, or in collision," a claim for particular average may be made, notwithstanding the clause. As a rule, this f.p.a. clause is used only when the goods are of such a nature as may be damaged by salt water or great heat.

Balance. The difference between the sides of an account; the amount necessary to close an account.

Balance Sheet. A brief summary, showing the balances of accounts, and whether a person or firm is solvent or insolvent.

Bank Rate. The rate per cent charged by the Bank of England for discounting bills.

Bankrupt. One unable to pay his debts in full (that is, where Liabilities exceed Assets) is *insolvent*; he is bankrupt when declared so by the Court.

Barter. To exchange one commodity directly for another.

Bill of Entry. A written statement of goods entered at a custom house, whether imported or for exportation.

Bill of Exchange. An unconditional order in writing, addressed by one person to another, for the payment of a specified sum of money, at a fixed date, to some person named, or to the bearer. A twopenny stamp is required on all bills.

Bill of Lading. A written statement, signed by the master or agents of a vessel, acknowledging the receipt of goods on board, and agreeing, under certain conditions, to deliver them safe to the person to whom they are directed. Such bills are transferable, like Bills of Exchange, or cheques, by endorsement.

Bill of Sale. An agreement under seal, by which a person conveys his title to property. The transaction must be *bona fide*, and the bill duly registered.

Bonded Goods. Imported goods left in a bonded warehouse until the duties are paid. Such goods are said to be *in bond*.

Bonus. A premium on a loan, or for any favour shown. An extra dividend to shareholders, etc.

Book Debts. All amounts owing *to* or *by* a merchant, as shown in his books.

Broker. A person whose business it is to negotiate or make sales and purchases for a commission, on behalf of other persons.

Brokerage. The commission payable to a broker for his services.

Capital. The amount invested in a business; the excess of the Assets over the Liabilities.

Carriage. The charge for conveying goods from one place to another, usually applied to goods sent by rail.

Cartage. Charges for hauling goods, usually to or from docks.

Charter Party. A contract entered into between the owner and the hirer of a vessel, for a certain period, or voyage, at an agreed rate, together with other particulars.

Cheque. An order upon a particular banker to pay a certain specified sum of money to a person named, or to bearer. Each cheque bears a twopenny stamp or frank mark, and cheque books are supplied by banks to those of their customers having current accounts, who are debited with the value of the stamp duty.

C.I.F. "Cost, insurance, and freight"; a price for goods which includes prime cost of goods, and insurance and freight charges of same to destination. Often pronounced "siff."

Commission. A charge made by a person who acts as an agent for another, usually a percentage.

Composition. A payment of something less than the full amount owing, made by a person who is insolvent or bankrupt, to settle the claim; the payment is usually at so much in the pound.

Consignee. The person to whom goods are sent.

Consignment. Goods sent to an agent to be sold on commission.

Consignment Note. A document to be filled up by the consignor when sending goods by railway.

Consignor. The sender of goods.

Credit. To put on the Cr. side of an account; credit sales are sales on trust, the goods to be paid for at a later time.

Credit Note. A note sent to a person stating that such person is credited with the amount quoted; usually given when goods are returned, or as an immediate allowance off payment, at a future date. See DEBIT NOTE.

Creditor. One to whom anything is owing.

Customs. Taxes charged by a Government upon goods imported from or exported to a foreign country. See BONDED GOODS.

Days of Grace. The three extra days always allowed for the payment of a bill. The custom is sanctioned by Act of Parliament. When the last day of grace falls on Sunday, Christmas Day, Good Friday, or a day appropriated by Royal Proclamation as a public fast or thanksgiving day, the bill is due and payable on the *preceding* business day; but when the last day of grace is a Bank Holiday (other than Christmas Day or Good Friday), or when the last day of grace is a Sunday, and the second day of grace is a Bank Holiday, the bill is due and payable on the *succeeding* business day.

Debenture. A certificate for money advanced to a company. Debentures have a first charge after mortgages, if any, for both the principal and the interest due on them on the whole of the assets of the undertaking. Accordingly they rank before the Preference and Ordinary capital.

Debit. To put on the Dr. side of an account.

Debit Note. A statement giving brief particulars of an amount charged to a person's account, and sent to him at the time the charge is made. See CREDIT NOTE.

Debtor. One who owes.

Demurrage. (1) The detention of a vessel beyond her specified time of sailing; (2) the compensation claimed or allowed for such delay; (3) A charge made by railway companies for detention of trucks, wagons, etc.; legal holidays and Sundays are not counted.

Deposit A/c. A sum of money, other than a current account, placed in a bank on deposit at interest. It can be withdrawn by giving the agreed number of days' notice.

Deposit Slip. A form used when depositing money in a bank.

Depreciation. The falling off in the value of machinery, plant, buildings, and other assets.

Discount. An amount deducted from an account; usually for prompt payment.

Discounting a Bill. To receive money from a banker for a bill before it is due. The banker's charge is called *discount*.

Dishonoured Bill. A bill which is not met, that is, paid, by the acceptor, when it falls due is said to be dishonoured.

Dishonouring a Bill. Failing to pay when the bill is presented for payment at maturity.

Dividend. (1) The portion allotted to each shareholder in the division of profits; (2) Instalments paid by a bankrupt estate to the creditors.

Double Entry. The entry of each transaction *twice* in the Ledger.

Draft. A bill, usually so called before it is accepted.

Draw. To draw upon a person is to send him a bill for acceptance.

Drawback. The amount of money "drawn back" from the Government on goods sold to customers abroad upon exportation, and on which goods the *Customs or Excise Duty* had been previously paid. See CUSTOMS.

Drawee. The person upon whom a bill is drawn.

Drawer. The person who *draws*, or *makes* the bill.

Duty. Charges made by the Government on import goods or on home manufactures subject to such duty.

E.E., E. & O.E. Errors Excepted; Errors and Omissions Excepted. Often written on invoices and accounts so that if any errors or omissions be afterwards discovered, the invoice may be corrected.

Endorse. To *sign* on the *back* of a bill or cheque when it is negotiated or paid away to another person.

Endorsee. The person to whom a bill, cheque, or other document is transferred by endorsement. He can then deal with the document as if it had been actually made out to him in the first instance.

Exchange. (1) A place where business interests of a special character are brought together, such as the *Stock* Exchange, *Corn* Exchange, etc. (2) A term applied to the method of remitting money from one country to another by means of bills instead of sending actual coin. The *"Par of Exchange"* is the equivalence of a given amount of the currency of one country which in *intrinsic* or *real value* is equal to a given sum in the currency of another country. The Rate or *"Course of Exchange"* is the sum of money in one country which, on any particular day, will exchange for any given sum, on the same day, in the currency of another country. The "Course of Exchange" will vary from day to day either above or below the "Par of Exchange." The latter never varies.

Free on Board (F.O.B.). A price charged or quoted for goods which shall include all expenses for delivery of the goods on board the ship.

Freight. (1) Charges for carrying goods by *water*; (2) The cargo of a ship.

Folio. The page of a book; the Dr. and Cr. sides of the Cash Book together form a folio.

Guarantee. A security for the performance of a contract; a security against loss.

Honouring a Bill. Paying it promptly when presented at maturity.

Insurance. A contract by which insurance offices agree to make good, to the party insuring, losses he may sustain of ships or cargoes at sea, or of houses or goods by fire, etc. The parties who take this risk are called the "insurers" or "underwriters"; the person protected is called the "insured"; the amount paid to the insurers is called the "premium"; and the written contract is called the "policy of insurance."

Interest. A charge made by the lender of money, on those who borrow; or on renewing a bill for a further period. Also the charge made upon a business by the partners in a firm for the use of capital invested by them in such business. Interest is usually charged at so much per cent per annum.

Investment. The amount of money laid out in the purchase of shares, houses, land, or other property, and on which a return is expected as interest or profit.

Invoice. The particulars of the quantity and prices of goods sold are given on an invoice.

IOU. "I owe you." A written statement acknowledging a debt, and consisting of these three letters, the amount of the debt, the signature of the debtor, and date. This document does not require a stamp, unless there is a promise to pay, in which case it becomes a promissory note.

Ledger. The book to which the entries in the Cash Book, Purchases Book, etc., are posted. The Ledger contains an abstract of all the other books.

Liabilities. Debts of a person or firm.

Limited Liability. A term meaning that the shareholders of a limited liability company are not liable for any sum in excess of the unpaid amount of the shares they have agreed to take. Thus, if I apply for and am allotted twenty £1 shares in X Ltd., my total liability is £20; even if the company is wound up I cannot be called upon to pay anything more.

Liquidation. The realization of the assets and the settling of the liability of a business or company; especially of a bankrupt.

Maturity of a Bill. The date when the bill is payable.

Mortgage. A grant of property made by the owner to a person lending him money on the security of such property. Such property is said to be *mortgaged*, the person to whom the mortgage is given being the *mortgagee*, and the one who gives the mortgage the *mortgagor*.

Negotiable. Transferable Bills are negotiable; that is, they may be transferred from one to another, and at the time a bill becomes due the holder of it has the rightful claim to the money.

Net. The amount remaining after all deductions, allowances, or discounts have been made.

Net Cash. A term applied to a bill for goods, to be paid without any allowances or discount, and without reference to time.

Net Proceeds. The amount remaining after all charges, expenses, and commission have been deducted.

Nominal or Fictitious Account. An account opened simply for the record of gains or losses, as the Profit and Loss Account.

Notary Public. A public officer who attests or certifies deeds and other writings. His duties chiefly relate to documents used in commercial transactions, such as protests of Bills of Exchange, etc.

Open Account. An unsettled account.

Par. The original amount paid for Stocks and Shares. When this price *rises*, they are said to be at a *premium*, or *above par*. Should the price, however, fall *below* the original amount, they are said to be at a *discount*, or *below par*.

Partner. Each individual person in a firm who has an interest or investment in such business.

Partnership. When two or more persons unite to carry on a particular business for purposes of profit, such union is called a partnership.

Personal Account. A record of transactions with persons.

Post-date. To date after the real time; that is, a date which has yet to arrive.

Postages Book. The book in which are recorded (1) on the Debit side, all receipts of postage stamps and (2) on the Credit side, all expenditures of postage stamps. The book is normally ruled to show the date, details of packages or the name of the addressee and the amount of postage on each article. The main advantages of keeping such a book are that it provides a ready check on the value of stamps in hand and is also a useful record of the date of posting any particular letter or parcel.

Posting. The term used to indicate the transferring of entries from the subsidiary books to the Ledger.

Price Current. A regularly published list of the market prices of goods.

Principal. (1) The head of a firm. (2) The amount of money lent out at interest.

Promissory Note. An unconditional promise, in writing, made by one person to another, signed by the maker, engaging to pay, on demand, or at a fixed determinable future time, a sum certain in money to, or to the order of, a specified person, or to bearer. A Promissory Note does not require *acceptance*, since it is *drawn* and is *payable* by the same person. In other respects, it is much the same as a Bill of Exchange.

Protest. (1) The steps taken to charge an endorser with liability for the payment of dishonoured commercial paper; (2) A written declaration sworn to by the master of a vessel, setting forth the cause of, and circumstances attending, damage to the vessel or cargo.

Purchases Book. The book in which are recorded the purchases on credit.

Real Account. An account of property of any kind; as Goods, Cash, Houses, etc.

Rebate. An amount deducted from the regular price; a discount or allowance.

Remittance. Commercial paper, or money, transmitted to another.

Reserve Fund. The proportion of profits of a business set aside for future unexpected losses, or to increase the working capital or financial strength of the company or firm.

Retiring a Bill. Honouring it, paying it when due.

Sales Book. The book in which are recorded the Sales on Credit.

Schedule. An inventory or catalogue of goods, with prices.

Shipping Note. A printed form to be filled up when goods are shipped.

Sighting a Bill. Accepting a bill which is drawn payable so many days or months after *sight*. The term of the bill is only reckoned from the date of *sighting* or *acceptance*. The *date* of *acceptance* must, therefore, be put on the bill, along with the signature of the acceptor.

Sinking Fund. A fund provided by setting aside and investing at arranged periods a sum of money which, with interest accumulated, will provide sufficient to replace an asset or meet a liability at a future fixed date.

Solvent. Able to pay all debts; that is, where the Assets exceed Liabilities.

Statement of Account. A periodical account showing the amounts due by one person or firm to another for goods supplied.

Stock. Raw material from which anything is made; goods in store and kept for sale; the capital represented by shares of a bank, or manufacturing or trading company or corporation held by individuals; a fund consisting of a capital debt due by Government to individual holders, who receive a rate of interest.

Stock-in-trade. The quantity and value of goods and merchandise which a dealer or manufacturer has in store at any particular time.

Stock-taking. A periodical valuation of all stock-in-trade, necessary for profit and loss purposes in balancing the books, and to enable a firm to ascertain their exact amount of capital.

Storage. Amount charged for keeping goods in a warehouse.

Suspense Account. An account in which items are entered temporarily until their proper "heading" is known.

Tare. An allowance made to the purchaser by deducting from the gross weight the weight of the case, cask, bag, or chest in which the goods are packed.

Tariff. A schedule or table of customs payable on merchandise, specifying the various duties charged on goods imported and articles exported, the drawbacks and bounties, etc., allowed.

Term of a Bill. The time allowed for payment, as "One month after date."

Trade Discount. The difference between the wholesale and retail prices.

Trade Price. The reduced price charged by wholesale to retail dealers so that the latter can make a profit on selling at the manufacturer's list price.

Usance. A certain period of time which it is the usage of different countries to allow for the payment of bills of exchange drawn upon them, exclusive of days of grace.

Voucher. Any material thing such as a writing that serves to attest an alleged act, especially that which serves to attest the payment of money, a receipt.

Wages Book. The book in which are recorded all the details necessary to the calculation of the net wages payable to individual employees. Columns are provided for each employee's Works or Payroll No., Name, No. of hours worked, Rate per hour and Gross wages and also for deductions such as National Insurance, Income Tax, etc. The final column shows the net amount payable to the employee.

Warrant. A receipt, in full detail, for goods deposited in a warehouse. A warrant is transferable by endorsement.

Watering Stock. Issuing additional stock without making additional provision for the payment of interest on the same; or increasing the nominal value of securities without a corresponding payment in cash.

Wharfage. The fee charged for the use of a wharf in discharging a vessel of her cargo.

Wharfinger. The owner or the person in charge of a wharf.

Without Engagement. A term sometimes used when quoting prices, and signifying that the person quoting does not bind himself to accept an order at the price named in the quotation.

Without Recourse to Me. Signifies that the endorser is not liable as such, if he has written these words over his signature.

Write Back. To cancel. In renewing a bill, the old one must first be "written back" or cancelled, and a fresh one will then be issued, usually for a higher amount, the interest for an extension of time, together with expenses incurred, having been added to the original amount.

Write Off. (1) To close a Ledger Account by transferring the difference as a Loss either to Discount and Allowances Account, or to a Bad Debts (or similar) account. (2) To reduce the book value of an asset.

INDEX